Ten Muslims

by

WILLIAM McELWEE MILLER

WILLIAM B. EERDMANS PUBLISHING COMPANY
GRAND RAPIDS, MICHIGAN

This book is dedicated to

THE CHURCH OF JESUS CHRIST IN IRAN

CONTENTS

FOREWORD

The biographical sketches in this volume were compiled by the Reverend William McElwee Miller, who served for 43 years as a notable evangelistic missionary in Iran. He is quite properly the author of this book, since he selected the personalities to be included and much the greater part of the material is from his hand. In some cases he has drawn on printed material or translations of original documents written by Iranian Christians. Where this is true, Dr. Miller has made it clear by footnotes or in the text itself. In addition, quotations are included from the letters and other writings of contemporary missionaries, of both the Presbyterian Mission and the Church Missionary Society. It is a privilege to be in this group, and also to have been asked to condense the material for publication and to do some necessary editing. To have a part in this project is all the more welcome, because Dr. Miller has been a close friend since seminary days and was my colleague in Iran for nearly twenty years. Also, I am fortunate to have known personally all but three of those whose stories are narrated.

The reader will note that the lives of some of those converts from Islam chosen for this volume extend well back into the 19th century. It was through their deep conviction of Jesus Christ as Savior and their fearless witness to this truth that the indigenous church in Iran was founded and has begun to grow. This has taken place mainly during the decades following the First World War. To accomplish this seemingly impossible task, the pioneers of the faith in Iran felt compelled to make use of controversy in the face of unalloyed fanaticism. We must be hesitant to judge them in this, but instead should be thankful that today there is greater openness in Iran, enabling both missionaries and indigenous Christians to present Christianity to Muslims through persuasion rather than by argument.

The life sketches in the following pages provide proof of the power of the Holy Spirit and assurance that, even under the most difficult circumstances, "the true Gospel . . . is coming to men the whole world over; everywhere it is growing and bearing fruit" (Colossians 1:6, New English Bible translation).

—WILLIAM NORRIS WYSHAM

INTRODUCTION

The world had entered the nineteenth century of the Christian era, which in the providence of God was to become the greatest century of Christian missionary outreach since the age of the apostles. William Carey had gone to preach Christ to the people of India. A few years later, 1807, a brilliant young scholar from Cambridge University, named Henry Martyn, arrived in India with the longing to "burn out for God." Taking on his heart the millions of Muslims of India and the Near East, Martyn undertook the translation of the New Testament into three of the languages used by Muslims — Arabic, Hindustani, and Persian.

As a result of overwork and inadequate nourishment, Martyn contracted tuberculosis, and his doctor recommended a sea voyage to improve his health. So the sick man journeyed to Persia, in the hope that, with the help of native scholars, he might perfect his translation of God's Word. In 1811 he came to Shiraz, where in ten months he completed his Persian translation of the New Testament. On the way back to England, Martyn died at Tokat in Turkey. He had indeed burned out for God. The original copy of his translation was published in 1815 by the Russian Bible Society and a year later by Carey's associates in Serampore, India. It became the basis for the Persian version in use today. Some years later, in 1848, the Old Testament was translated by William Glen and the whole Bible was made available in the Persian language. Without the Bible, any effort to evangelize the Muslims of Persia would have proved futile.

But the Bible, without men and women to put it into the hands of the people and to make known its truths by word and deed, is like bread locked in a storeroom in time of famine. Who in Persia would take the Bread of Life to hungry people? There were many Christians in the country at that time. In the northwest lived thousands of Nestorians, now known as Assyrians, remnants of the Syriac-speaking Church of the East, which had once taken the Gospel across Asia to China. It survived, but had become a weak minority in a Muslim land. It had lost its missionary zeal and made no effort to evangelize the Jews and Muslims who surrounded it. Also, there were Armenian Christians in parts of Persia but, like the Assyrians, they had suffered much for their faith, knew little of the teachings of the

6

Bible, and had no concern for the salvation of their non-Christian neighbors. There were also a few Roman Catholics in Persia, known as Chaldeans. It was certain that rarely would any of these native Christians dare to distribute and teach the Persian Scriptures to the Muslims.

But God put it into the hearts of Christians in other lands to bring God's Word to the Persian people. German members of the Basle Mission came to Tabriz in northwest Persia in 1825. After working zealously for twelve years, they moved on to India. One of them, Dr. C. G. Pfander, wrote powerful controversial books, the best known of which is *The Balance of Truth* (1836), a book that played a part in the conversion of several of those whose stories are told in this volume.

Shortly before the German missionaries left Persia, the pioneers of the American "Mission to the Nestorians" arrived in Tabriz in 1834. A year later they settled in Urumia (Rezaieh), west of Lake Rezaieh. The Reverend and Mrs. Justin Perkins, sent out by the American Board in Boston, had official instructions that their "main object will be to enable the Nestorian Church, through the grace of God, to exert a commanding influence in the spiritual regeneration of Asia." They, and the noble men and women who later joined them, labored and prayed that the Nestorian Church might come to life. As a result, many Assyrians became living witnesses to the power of Christ, though the hope of the missionaries was not fully realized.

In 1835, the American Board sent the Reverend James Merrick to Persia on a "Mission to the Mohammedans." In company with members of the Basle Mission, he went to Teheran and thence to Isfahan, where the city was thrown into confusion when they gave copies of Christian books to Muslims, and their lives were threatened. After visiting several cities and finding strong opposition from Muslims everywhere, he wrote to the Board, "I am at length convinced that public preaching to the Persians is at present, not only inexpedient, but impracticable." As a result of his report, the "Mission to the Mohammedans" was discontinued.

However, the work of the "Mission to the Nestorians" was continued and enlarged. In 1870 this mission became a "Mission to Persia," and was transferred to the Presbyterian Church in the U.S.A. New centers were opened over a period of forty years in Teheran, Tabriz, Hamadan, Resht, Kermanshah, and Meshed. Schools and hospitals were established in these cities. Many Muslims came as patients to the hospitals, and gradually Muslim pupils began to enroll in the Christian schools. In this way much hostility and misunderstanding was dissipated, as Jews and Muslims came into friendly contact with the missionaries and with the members of the evangelical churches that had been established in all the centers of the Mission. At first most of those who in the newer centers united with the evangelical churches were Armenians, some of whom, like the Assyrians in Urumia, became effective Christian witnesses. The Bible was now made available to many people by the missionaries, and later by the tireless labors of the colporteurs of the British and Foreign Bible Society. Here and there Muslims began to read the Word of God, to talk with Christians, and to seek for the truth.

In 1869 the Reverend Robert Bruce, a missionary of the Church Missionary Society of the Anglican Church, came to Isfahan and there established the work of his church. He later became the revisor of the Persian Bible. Several Muslims came to Mr. Bruce and expressed a desire to become Christians, but when two men were beheaded by the authorities for attending a Christian church service, it became clear that religious freedom had not yet come to Persia. The Anglican Mission, like the Presbyterian Mission in the north, established schools and hospitals in Isfahan, Shiraz, Kerman, and Yezd, and in central and south Persia the Gospel was made known to a great many people. A church was established in Isfahan, largely made up of Armenians. Later, churches were founded also in the other cities. Zoroastrians, Jews, and Muslims were converted and came into the church.

The churches in the north today, while still in fraternal relationship with The United Presbyterian Church in the U.S.A., have become an autonomous communion — the Evangelical Presbyterian Church of Iran, which is entirely responsible for its own administration, the care of its churches and evangelistic outreach. Missionaries, now called fraternal workers, assist the church in many ways and retain leadership in some of the educational and medical institutions. In the south, the church is part of the worldwide Anglican communion, with missionaries from Great Britain and other lands, but with a Muslim convert as its bishop.

Several other Protestant missions have done faithful work at various times and places in Persia. The work of the Roman Catholic Church has been directed especially towards the Christian minorities, and little has been done to evangelize Muslims. During the period with which we are concerned in this book, the chief agencies of evangelism were the Presbyterian and Anglican Missions and the churches they established, and the Bible Society through its depots and colporteurs.

The question has often been asked, "Why is it so difficult to convert Muslims, and why is the church so weak in most Muslim lands?" In reply we would remind the questioner that Islam is the only one of the great religions of the world that came into existence after the birth of Christ, which recognizes Christianity as having been the true religion in its day, and claims to have superseded Christianity as the one true religion of the world. Muslims believe that God is one, but refuse to call him "Father." They believe that God sent many prophets into the world to give men divine laws and guide them in the right way, the greatest being Noah, Abraham, Moses, Jesus, and Mohammed. They believe that God gave books to some of the prophets, and they have heard of the *Torat* of Moses, the *Zabur* of David, and the *Injil* of Jesus. However, they consider these books no longer necessary for men, since God's perfect will has been revealed in the Koran, the very Word of God, which was given to Mohammed.

The Koran tells of how Jesus was born to the Virgin Mary, but it denies His divine sonship. It also refers to Jesus' miracles of healing, and Muslims generally know that Jesus was given power by God even to raise the dead to life. But the Koran emphatically denies the death of Jesus on the cross, and it is usually thought that one of Jesus' enemies was changed by God to resemble Him, and was crucified by mistake in His place. Jesus, it is said, was taken alive to heaven, where He is today. It is generally supposed that Jesus in the *Injil* foretold the coming of Mohammed, and bade His followers to accept him when he appeared. But since there is no reference to Mohammed in the Christian Scriptures, Muslims often charge Christians with the crime of corrupting their holy books, saying that the predictions of the coming of Mohammed have been removed, and false statements have been inserted about Jesus as the Son of God and as crucified and raised from the dead.

The attitude of the majority of Muslims in a land like Iran is that while Jesus was a very great and good prophet, His place has been taken by Mohammed, the last and greatest of the prophets. Hence they say they do not want to "go backward" and become followers of Jesus. On the contrary, Christians in obedience to their Master should "go forward" and accept Mohammed and the Koran.

Moreover, Islam is not only a religion; it is a system of life in which political, social, economic, and religious elements are united, and even when a Muslim becomes convinced that Christ

9

is the only Savior, it is very difficult for him to profess his faith openly and break with his society. In Iran perhaps 98 percent of the population are Muslims, and the convert to Christianity feels very much alone.

In spite of the seemingly insuperable difficulties in the conversion of Muslims, in the providence of God there are today many hundreds of members in the Christian churches in Iran who once were Muslims, or who are the children of converts from Islam. It is now possible to baptize converts publicly in the churches. Some converts are faithfully serving as pastors and evangelists, and the bishop of the Anglican Church retains his Muslim name to demonstrate that it is possible in Iran for Muslims to confess openly their faith in Christ and serve him with boldness. However, the freedom which is enjoyed today, like religious freedom in other lands, was not achieved without courage and suffering. The fearless and faithful witness of men like Dr. Sa'eed, the subject of one of our stories, has been used by God, along with other factors, to bring in the day for which the pioneers prayed and waited.

Even though it is easier now than it once was in Persia and in some other lands for Muslims to become Christians, questions regarding the validity of the effort to evangelize Muslims are frequently asked: Have the results of missionary effort in Muslim lands justified the great expenditure of life and money? Since the religion of Islam teaches people to worship one God, and in many ways resembles the Christian faith, why should we attempt to convert Muslims to Christianity? If a Muslim should be attracted to Christ and wish to become His follower, why should he be encouraged to accept baptism and profess his faith openly, thereby cutting himself off from his Islamic society and culture, and bringing on himself persecution and even the danger of death? Can he not remain a secret believer and avoid all this suffering? Theological and Biblical answers have been given to these difficult questions, but it is also important that we listen to the testimony of people who left Islam and became members of the Christian church. The lives and words of the sincere believers to whom the reader will be introduced in this book give eloquent and convincing answers to these questions.

* * * * *

An explanation is called for as to one or two terms used in this volume. The spelling "Muslim," instead of "Moslem," the common spelling in English, is used for the adherent of Islam. In this introduction, Persia has been used as the name of the land which is the scene of our stories, for, until forty years ago,

10

it was so identified outside the country. But after Reza Shah Pahlevi came to the throne, he asked other nations to call his country by the name used by its people, so Persia is now Iran, which means "The Land of the Aryans." In the chapters to follow, it will be called by that name, without regard to the date involved.

Likewise a suggestion as to the pronunciation of Persian names may be helpful to the reader, especially if he desires to quote from this book. The accent on Persian proper names is on the last syllable, The "kh" sound is like "ch" in "loch"; the "q" like a guttural "g". The following may assist in pronouncing the more difficult names among the subjects of our stories: Kaka (Kah-ka); Sa'eed; Nozad (No-zahd); Merat-us-Sultan (Mer-aht-us-Sultahn); Jalil Qazzaq (Ja-leel Qaz-zahq); Khadijeh (Khad-e-jeh); Jalily (Ja-lee-lee).

The stories of the devoted Christians herein recorded have been compiled from material written as a labor of love and an expression of gratitude by the following persons who knew them and loved them and were blessed and inspired by their loyalty to Jesus Christ: Miss Nouhie Aiden, The Reverend and Mrs. Cady H. Allan, The Rt. Reverend Hassan B. Dehqani-Tafti, Miss Vera Eardley, The Reverend John Elder, The Reverend Jollynoos S. Hakim, Mrs. Sarah McDowell, The Reverend and Mrs. William M. Miller, Mr. J. D. Payne, The Rt. Reverend J. H. Richards, The Reverend William N. Wysham.

WILLIAM McELWEE MILLER

Mt. Airy, Philadelphia, Pa.

11

● Bokhara   ● Samarkand

V I ET U N I O N
Turkestan

● Eshkabad

Sarakhs

● Meshed
Nishapur

● Torbat

● Herat

A F G H A N I S T A N

N

● Quetta

Zahedan ●

P A K I S T A N

B a l u c h i s t a n

of Oman   Arabian Sea

1

Two Brothers in Kurdistan

In the northwest of Iran lies the eastern end of a crescent called Kurdistan that extends over into northern Iraq and southeastern Turkey. Its inhabitants are known as Kurds, a people of Aryan extraction who have preserved to a large extent their racial purity, language, and customs. They are of a sturdy stock, famed in the past for their liberal hospitality, their religious fanaticism, and their warlike propensities. The part of Kurdistan lying in Iran is one of the fourteen main provinces of the country and is located in the heart of the Zagros mountain range that runs along the border of Iraq. It is a land of exceeding beauty, with snow-clad mountain peaks, yawning ravines with turbulent streams, and scattered valleys green with springtime vegetation.

The main city of Kurdistan and the capital of the province is Sanandaj (Senneh in ordinary parlance), a place of moderate size, a center of trade for the surrounding villages, and a locality where Muslim theologians used to gather. In this fanatical city in the middle of the nineteenth century lived Rasool and his family in a small three-room house.* He was the seventh in a long line of well-known Muslim ecclesiastics; hence he was called Mulla** Rasool. He maintained himself and his family by writing prayers for the sick, by treating all sorts of disease, by instructing the newly buried how to answer the two angels that come, according to Muslim doctrine, to catechize them as .to their religious belief, and by conducting a school to teach twenty to thirty boys Persian and Arabic. He led the daily prayers at a nearby mosque. With no fear of contagion, he went

* Most of the facts and incidents in Chapters I and III are taken from the book, *Dr. Sa'eed of Iran,* by Jay Rasooli, son of Mohammed Rasooli, and published by Grand Rapids International Publications, 1957. This material is used with their permission.

** A mulla is a cleric of the Muslim religion.

from time to time to visit a leper colony outside the city to comfort the poor wretches in their misery.

Mulla Rasool and his wife, a very worthy and competent woman, had eight children. One after another died till only two boys were left, Mohammed, the elder, and Sa'eed, eight years younger. According to Kurdish custom, Sa'eed, as the younger of the two, never addressed Mohammed by name, but always called him "Kaka," the word for "brother" in their language. Consequently, when they moved away from their native province to a locality where Kurdish was not spoken and people heard Sa'eed call his brother "Kaka," they followed his custom, and so everyone got to know him as "Kaka." For this reason, he will be referred to henceforth by that name. Though full blood brothers, the difference in their surnames is due to the fact that in the early days people had only one name. Many years later, when the two brothers were well advanced in years, the government required all its subjects to adopt family names. So Kaka chose his father's name and Sa'eed his native province, each adding an *i* to indicate origin: hence, Mohammed Rasooli and Sa'eed Kurdistani.

In 1876 Mulla Rasool died, leaving Kaka at the age of twenty-one as head of the family. Though Sa'eed was only thirteen at the time, he had acquired such an amazing knowledge of Persian and Arabic, as well as the Koran, that the people who gathered at the memorial service of Mulla Rasool endowed him with the title of a mulla and chose him to take over his father's school. As head of the family, Kaka now became responsible for its maintenance. So he had to give up the studies that he was pursuing and earn money by reading the Koran aloud at shrines and graves.

Both Kaka and Sa'eed were ardent Muslims in the stronghold of fanaticism where they lived. They were faithful in attending the mosques, in saying their ritual prayers five times a day, and in refraining from food and drink from dawn to dusk during the month of Ramazan, as required by Islamic regulations.

In 1834 two Protestant missionaries had come to Iran to work among the Assyrians in the city of Urumia (now Rezaieh) in the northwest corner of the country. In the course of forty years of missionary work, a strong Protestant movement had set foot in Urumia and the surrounding area, with churches and schools both in the city and adjacent villages. Pastors and teachers had been trained, and they were sending out evangelists and Bible colporteurs to other cities.

In the year 1879, when Kaka was twenty-four and Sa'eed

16

sixteen, an evangelist, Kasha Yohanan,* and two Bible colporteurs arrived in Senneh to sell Scriptures and to propagate the Christian faith. The colporteurs were making a short visit, but Kasha Yohanan was planning a long stay. In order to improve his use of Persian, which was not the vernacular in his part of the country, he was looking for a teacher. In response to his inquiries Sa'eed was recommended. After securing permission from Kaka as head of the family, Sa'eed undertook the desired instruction. Their textbook, so far as they had any, was the Bible.

From the very first, Sa'eed watched the conduct of these three men, for he had heard so much that was derogatory of Christians that he was strongly prejudiced against them. But he found that the accusations he had heard certainly did not apply in the case of these three. They did not use liquor, they were honest, they even prayed for their enemies. He had to revise his opinions.

In due time the colporteurs continued their journey, leaving Sa'eed alone with Kasha Yohanan. Reading from the Bible, they often discussed religion. Sa'eed had many questions. He even began studying Syriac, the language of the Assyrians, to compare the Bible translations. Kasha Yohanan gave him a Syriac New Testament, which he showed to his brother. Kaka was angry and warned him against the book, lest it lead him astray. However, this did not restrain Sa'eed, but made him feel he must continue his investigation, but secretly. He studied especially the Messianic prophecies in the Old Testament and could not see how they were fulfilled in Mohammed. Eventually he took a Bible home and showed it to Kaka and begged that he might keep on with its study in order to write a refutation of Christianity. Kaka was pleased and granted permission. He could now study the Bible openly.

The more Sa'eed studied and the more he became acquainted with Kasha Yohanan and observed his Christian character, the more doubts began to arise in his mind as to his Muslin faith. One day on his way to the mosque for evening prayers the thought flashed into his mind, "What if Mohammed was not a true prophet?" This blasphemous suggestion so shocked him that he felt himself unclean and under a curse. He hurried on to the mosque, hoping to wash away the contamination of his mind by his ablutions, but his heart found no peace.

Returning home, he retired early but sleep would not come. Finally, he arose with the firm determination to settle the matter

* *Kasha* is the Syriac word used for an ordained minister and *Yohanan* is Syriac for "John."

17

once for all. He lighted a fire and with a pair of tongs lifted
out a live coal. This he pressed against one leg and then against
the other. The pain was agonizing but he did not flinch till
deep wounds were made. When they finally healed, they left
two permanent scars — one to remind him of the vow he had
just made, never to speak to Christians again about religion,
the other to bring to his mind his disgraceful conduct in doubt-
ing his Muslim faith and to help him avoid evil in the future. It
was in accordance with Kurdish custom in taking a vow to
make a scar on the body as a reminder to keep the undertaking.

Having thus made his resolve and having sealed it with
wounds, he sent word to Kasha Yohanan that pressure of work
would not permit him to continue his teaching.

But this failed to relieve him. The doubts persisted. The
wounds healed but not the heart. One night, on returning from
the mosque, he prostrated himself in a dark corner and with
tears besought God to deliver him from his misery and lead him
in the right way. Even as he prayed, the weight seemed to lift,
and he determined to study both Bible and Koran and to resume
his studies with Kasha Yohanan.

For some months he pursued this course, studying the Bible
under the pastor's guidance, and the Koran with the help of
commentaries. In the latter he found nothing to assuage his
thirst.

As Sa'eed spent more time with Kasha Yohanan, Kaka became suspicious and reproved him with harsh words. He
boasted of Mohammed and spoke derisively of Christians. One
day he even beat Sa'eed, breaking several sticks in the process.
Sa'eed fell to the ground and kissed the earth at Kaka's feet.

Not long after this Sa'eed was sitting in the pastor's room,
sad because of the impending departure of his friend, when
suddenly there rang in his heart the words of Isaiah: "Arise,
shine, for thy light is come, and the glory of the Lord is risen
upon thee" (Isaiah 60:1). These words reverberated within
him until his whole person seemed to fill with happiness. Kasha
Yohanan saw this and asked the reason. Sa'eed told him, and
after prayers of thanksgiving, the pastor said to him: "Rejoice,
for you have found grace with God."

After a few days Kasha Yohanan took his departure, urging
his young friend to be diligent in prayer, lest he be tempted to
turn back from his new found faith, in which case it would be
better that he had never accepted Christianity. This admonition
Sa'eed never forgot.

Now, all alone, he faced a dilemma. Should he confess his
new faith? Death would probably ensue. Should he take refuge

18

in flight? That would be hard to accomplish. He decided to solve his problem by dissimulation. He would go up on the rooftop of the mosque and give the call to prayer, but after crying out the words, "I testify that Mohammed is the Apostle of God," he would pray in an undertone, "O God, forgive me." Then he would go down and join the people at prayers, but in place of saying the prescribed sentences as he followed the genuflections and prostrations, he would whisper the Lord's Prayer or the Apostles' Creed. But this double life was heartbreaking to one so sincere.

At last he could stand it no longer. One of his intimate friends was a young man, Faizullah by name. On a Friday after the prayers were over, while Sa'eed and Faizullah lingered on the roof of the mosque, Sa'eed took the opportunity to tell his companion of his newfound faith. Day after day they conversed together, Faizullah trying to win his friend back to Islam. When he found it was useless, he tried to cheer him by diverting his thoughts to other things. One day Faizullah invited Sa'eed and a few companions to his father's garden. While tea was in preparation, the young men amused themselves by singing songs, but Sa'eed had no heart for such entertainment. Taking some bread, he stepped out into the vineyard and engaged in prayer. He ate the bread, plucked some of the grapes, and meditated on the death of Christ. It was his first Lord's Supper!

Gradually he let his secret be known to other friends. There was no special danger in this, for they would have no wish to expose him. The trouble came from another source. A Jewish doctor asked him if he would like to learn Hebrew as well as Syriac. He said he would, so it was agreed that he teach the physician's children Persian in return for Hebrew from their father. The doctor had many Jewish friends with whom Sa'eed engaged in religious conversation. Unable to answer his arguments, they became angry and spread abroad the word that Sa'eed had become a Christian.

Quickly the rumor spread. On the streets some people reviled him. Others he could hear saying, "There goes the accursed fellow." Except for close friends and some of the Catholics in the city there was none to sympathize.

In these days there returned to the city from a trip to Russia a God-fearing Catholic merchant, on whom Sa'eed went to call, since the man was a friend of Kasha Yohanan. To him Sa'eed reported his conversion. He, in turn, asked Sa'eed if he was ready to face the dangers involved, to which Sa'eed replied that not even martyrdom could make him forsake Christ. Thereupon the merchant presented him with some books; among them was Pfander's *The Balance of Truth,* written in refutation of Islam and translated into Persian. But these books he had to read in secret and keep hidden lest Kaka discover them.

As yet Sa'eed had not told his brother of his change of faith, but from the fact that he no longer said his morning prayers nor read the Koran, Kaka realized that some important change had taken place. So, by boasts of Mohammed and talk of "Christian dogs," by threats and beatings, he and his friends sought to force Sa'eed to resume his previous practices. Once Sa'eed attempted to flee from the city, but his intentions were found out and his plan failed.

One day the chief mulla of the city sent for Sa'eed and asked him to bring a Bible, with the request that he show him some passages with which he was familiar. Upon examining the book he said he could find nothing in it to cause Muslims to hate Christians. Sa'eed was greatly pleased, but then he made a serious mistake; he let him have Pfander's *The Balance of Truth*. The mulla was stirred to the quick and resolved to write a refutation, announcing in the chief mosque that the Shah had requested him to do so. At the same time, he was a kindly man and sought to protect Sa'eed from the local fanatics.

Once again Sa'eed endeavored to flee, this time under the protection of a visiting bishop who was going to Turkey, but he set out too late and failed to overtake his anticipated protector. So he returned, footsore and weary.

Winter now came on. The persecution he faced at home was about all he could bear. One day as Kaka, Sa'eed, and a neighbor were seated around the *kursi,** Sa'eed was reading to the others from a Muslim book about Mohammed's birth and the miraculous signs that attended it. Kaka started to speak in praise of such a marvelous prophet, whereupon Sa'eed made bold to suggest that if the stories were true, they should have been foretold, and hence it would be well to examine the Bible to see if it contained prophecies of Mohammed's coming. The neighbor agreed, but Kaka flew into a rage. He reached for the loaded rifle hanging on the wall and pointed at his brother, but the mulla intervened and seized the gun. He then took Sa'eed away and warned him to be more careful in what he said.

Sa'eed realized the danger he was in. What should he do? He thought again of flight, but two attempts had proved in vain.

* A *kursi* was a low, square table placed over a depression in the floor which held a brazier of burning coals. Over this was placed a large quilt and the family sat around it on cushions with the quilt drawn up around them.

Kaka was pressing him to know why he was so sad and pre-occupied. Finally, he decided to make confession, not by word of mouth, lest it rouse his brother to a frenzy, but in writing. So he wrote a letter, saying that he had long been a Christian and that he was ready to die for his faith, but if Kaka would spare him, he would be his servant for the rest of his life. For days he kept this letter in his pocket, hesitating to give it to his brother.

Finally, one night when the two brothers and a visitor were again sitting around the *kursi,* they started discussing religion. Kaka and the guest made remarks that Sa'eed could not bear to hear, so he went outside and knelt in prayer, beseeching God's help. On his return he took the letter from his pocket and gave it to his brother. From the look of anger on Kaka's face, the neighbor surmised the tenor of the letter and left in haste.

After Kaka had burned the letter, the two brothers lay down under the *kursi* for the night, but neither one could go to sleep. At last Kaka began speaking and with each sentence his rage increased, till he finally shouted:

"A dog and a man cannot live together. Clear out!"

"Where can I go on such a night?" entreated Sa'eed.

"What's that to me?"

"Please let me stay here tonight. I'll go tomorrow."

"Get out, you cursed dog!" Kaka reached for the gun.

Sa'eed quickly put on his clothes and stepped out into the bitter cold. He knocked on the doors of his Catholic friends, but they were afraid to take him in. At last he was accepted by an old woman for whom he had often written letters. So as not to get her into difficulty, he left early in the morning and went to his school to await what might happen.

Kaka spent the night crying to God, "You have taken my father and mother, and now my brother has left." Like Sa'eed he also rose early, took his rifle, and stationed himself in a shop opposite the Catholic church, where he surmised his brother had spent the night. When people asked him why he was there with his gun, he told them that Sa'eed had turned apostate and he was waiting to kill him. When they heard this, they cast aside all restraint and Kaka soon learned that thirty men had bound themselves to kill Sa'eed. However ready Kaka was to shoot Sa'eed himself, he was not ready to turn his only brother over to an angry mob.

He went to consult his stepmother's sister, a prudent and tenderhearted woman. Together they went to the school, where she brought about a kind of reconciliation. Kaka accepted his brother back into his home, and now as a Christian. It was a great victory for Sa'eed. Kaka also went to the leading mulla, as Sa'eed had done, reported the situation, and asked his advice what to do. "Do nothing," was the reply. "Leave it to me. I will bring him back to Islam with proofs from the Koran."

When the Muslims learned that Kaka was protecting his brother, they wanted to kill him, too. Conditions constantly became worse. One day in the spring came a letter for Sa'eed from the Reverend James W. Hawkes, a missionary in the city of Hamadan, eighty miles to the southeast. He had learned from a recent visit to Senneh of the danger the new convert was facing; and so he invited him to come to be his language teacher. Sa'eed pleaded with Kaka to let him go. Consent was finally given.

They planned that Sa'eed should join a caravan leaving for Hamadan. The two brothers would leave by different routes and join the caravan outside the city. Kaka carried Sa'eed's few belongings. After they had met at the appointed place, they came to a brook swollen with spring rains. They walked along its bank till they reached a place where it was possible to ford. Here Kaka lifted Sa'eed to his shoulders and carried him across. This one act did much to restore relations between the two brothers. They reached the caravan at sunset and bade each other goodbye.

About midnight the caravan started on, and it traveled till sunrise. Sa'eed now began to feel safe, when all of a sudden his hopes were shattered by the reappearance of Kaka with two friends, who had come to take him back. Kaka reported that the city was in turmoil. People were clamoring for Sa'eed's return and were threatening to tear down the family house. Kaka pleaded with Sa'eed to return, but Sa'eed was obdurate. "Kill me here if you will," he said, "I cannot return to the city." When Kaka saw that all effort to persuade his brother was useless, he embraced him and turned back. Sa'eed went on with the caravan and after five days reached Hamadan. This was in 1881.

A new life now opened up for Sa'eed. He was free from the fear of the fanatical Muslims of Senneh, he was living in the security of a missionary home, and was making acquaintance with Armenian and Jewish converts. He asked for baptism, but neither Mr. Hawkes nor the Hamadan Armenians thought it advisable, for it might stir up the Muslim community. At this juncture the Shah's brother, a ruthless despot, was appointed governor of Hamadan. The Armenians feared that Sa'eed's open confession of Christianity might bring trouble on them, so they desired that according to Muslim usage he should again shave his head and wear his turban, customs which he had set aside after his flight.

In the fall of his first year in Hamadan, a missionary physician, Dr. E. W. Alexander, arrived from America with his wife to set up practice in the city. Because of his rapid progress in English. Sa'eed became his interpreter and assistant. Through his contact with missionaries and other Christians, studying with Mr. Hawkes and attending Christian meetings, Sa'eed was growing spiritually. The thing that especially distressed him was that, since he had not been baptized, he was not allowed to partake of the Lord's Supper, though he had suffered more for his faith than any of the other Christians.

He had been in Hamadan about two and a half years when he was greatly cheered by a visit from Kaka, who seemed to have lost his old fanatical spirit and to look upon Sa'eed's conversion to Christianity as unchangeable. The two brothers had many discussions about religion in a friendly spirit before Kaka returned home.

After some time had elapsed, Kaka decided to visit Hamadan again. He sold the house and gave out that he was going to get Sa'eed and take him where he would recant his errors. Some of the people doubted this and to detain him offered to make him leader of prayers at the mosque he attended. After he had left, the mullas maintained that the house had belonged to an apostate and hence was forfeit to the mosque. Under the circumstances Kaka refunded the proceeds to the purchaser, making the sale a complete loss of both house and furnishings.

With Kaka now residing in Hamadan, the missionaries tried to persuade him to read the Bible. To this end they would give him a tract or Scripture passages to copy for pay. But when he came to lines he did not like, he might tear up the writing or jab it with the Kurdish dagger which he always carried in his sash. At such times they would urge him not to be agitated by the meaning of the passage, but to go on copying and earn his fee. Dr. Alexander was lending him books to read, among them *The Balance of Truth,* the volume which Sa'eed had given the Kurdistan mulla. As he read this book, he learned of God's judgment on sin and the message of Christ's love. It began to affect him. Day by day he went to the leading mosque but found no help from the preaching. What influenced him most was the contrast between the conduct of Muslims and the lives of the Christian missionaries and teachers. He started going to the daily prayers at Dr. Alexander's home and occasionally, with some trepidation, to church services.

23

The day came when one of the missionaries was returning to America and Kaka was asked to accompany him to the Iranian border. On the way he was thrown from his horse and broke his kneecap, an accident which left him with a stiff knee for the rest of his life. On his return to Hamadan, while convalescing from his injury, he had nothing to do but read. He studied the Bible in earnest and at last, greatly to Sa'eed's joy, was ready to make in no uncertain terms a confession of his faith in Christ. It had taken him a long time and careful study to reject Islam and accept Christianity, but once he had made his decision, there was no turning back.

From this point on, the lives of the two brothers from Kurdistan diverge. They had their own homes, their own families, their separate work. Each deserves a special chapter in our book.

2

Kaka, the Evangelist

After his conversion to the Christian faith and final departure from Kurdistan, Kaka had to find some regular employment in his new home in Hamadan. His first job was that of hostler for one of the missionaries. In those days there were no carriages or carriage roads in Hamadan and travel between cities was by caravan. To go from one town to another, people had to ride some kind of mount unless they chose to walk. So the missionaries kept horses. Thus it was that Kaka became a hostler and probably had other servant duties. To see this proud mulla serving in such a capacity makes one think of the One who "took upon him the form of a servant" (Phil. 2:7).

From this menial task he was promoted to be manager of a boys' dormitory. Mr. Hawkes had opened a school for boys, later taken over by the Reverend J. G. Watson. There were some Armenian boys that came from a distance and so a boarding school was opened for them. Because of its small size the duties of manager were not onerous.

After some years the school was discontinued. Kaka was now appointed an evangelist. He went through the city streets and bazaars distributing Christian literature. He sat in the waiting room of the dispensary, reading from the Bible or talking with the patients as they sat around in anticipation of their turn to see the doctor. He did similar work with patients in the hospital. As he walked the streets, he was at times greeted with harsh words, curses, or tongue lashings by a fanatical Muslims. On one occasion he was attacked by a wild Kurd with a dagger, who had mistaken him for his brother Sa'eed, but he was able to defend himself until others came to his aid.

Kaka's special delight, however, was to go on evangelistic trips to the villages around Hamadan. Sometimes he was accompanied by another evangelist. At other times there would be a lady evangelist and a lady missionary in addition to the men. Since there were no roads from village to village, travel was by donkeyback. The party would start out in the morning, probably arrive at the next village within an hour or two and find a house where they could stay. In winter they would sit around a *kursi*. If the ladies were along, they would, of course, need two rooms. If the owner of the house or some other villagers came in, the men would talk with them or read from the Bible. If no one came, they would go out in the streets or fields to find a group to talk to. At night several callers would probably gather at the house. Usually the people were friendly and listened with interest. Occasionally some fanatic would show up and wish to argue for his faith or even to threaten. Unless it was a large village or city, they stayed only one night and then moved on early the next morning. As villages were repeatedly visited, the people got to know Kaka and welcomed his coming.

On this village itineration he had many interesting experiences. One who often accompanied him on these trips reports that one day a man, seeing the evangelistic group ride by, ran through the fields, calling out, "Kaka! Kaka!" They stopped, waiting for the man to catch up. Kaka had a few words with him. Later, when out of the man's hearing, Kaka explained that this man was coming to see and hear him later in the day, for he was practically convinced of the truth of the Gospel. Yet some years before, he had kept Kaka from sleep one night, telling him that as an apostate he ought to be killed, though he was greatly impressed with Kaka's knowledge of the Bible and the Koran. Kaka had not become angry with him, but told him that he loved him and that God loved him, too. If, however, he felt it obligatory to kill him, let him go ahead. Kaka concluded by saying, "This man is one of my best friends today."

On another trip after he had finished reading from the New Testament and explaining it to a group of men, he asked a young man sitting next to him if he could read. He said he could. So Kaka handed him his Testament and told him to read. He took the book, turned it upside down, and began to move his lips. Kaka thought he was illiterate and pretending to read, so he told him to read out loud. He did so. "Why did you turn the book upside down?" asked Kaka. He replied: "In the village where I grew up there was just one man who was literate, a mulla. He gathered a group of us boys together to teach us to read, and he had us sit around him in a semicircle. There was only one book, which the mulla held on his lap. My place was right in front of him;

26

hence, I always saw the book upside down, and so that was the way I learned to read."

In the summer of 1935, when Kaka was almost eighty years of age, he and Sa'eed were reminiscing together one day. Their conversation went back to experiences in Kurdistan. Sa'eed indicated he would like to go to Senneh once more. "What about me?" said Kaka. "I haven't seen the city for over fifty years." The very next day came an urgent call by telephone for Sa'eed, now a doctor, to go to see the wife of the governor whom he had gone to Senneh to treat over twenty years before. At first he declined, for he knew it would be ministering not just to one person but seeing patients all day long, and he did not feel he had the strength for it. He finally consented, however, if his son-in-law, Dr. Tatevos, would accompany him. So he sent word to his brother to get ready to go with them. Kaka was elated.

Great was his joy to visit the city of his youth and see the places so replete with memories — the old home now in ruins, his parents' graves, the mosques he had attended. During the eight days his brother was busy seeing patients, he had ample time to get around. He was entertained day and night, and everywhere he went he testified freely to his Christian faith and distributed tracts.

On the day of their departure some of the dignitaries of the city gathered at the governor's residence to bid them farewell. One of the men, thinking to tease Kaka, said to him in the presence of the others: "Why do you want to go back to Hamadan? Stay here and return to Islam. We will find you a good wife and provide you with all the money you want."

"I have the gift of eternal life," said Kaka. "What do I care for this world's riches? If you would fill this large palace with gold coins, it would not tempt me!"

"Why, then, did you persecute your brother, going after him with a gun with the intent to kill him?"

"That was in the days of my ignorance, just as you today fail to understand the gift of eternal life in Christ." Such was Kaka's parting confession of his faith to the people of Senneh, where years before he had sought to kill his brother for giving the same testimony.

It was only a short time after his return to Hamadan that he suffered a stroke of paralysis which sent him to the hospital. After some months he made a wonderful recovery. Unable to converse with people because of his extreme deafness, he still could walk the streets, and this he did two hours a day, handing out tracts.

27

On one of these daily excursions he was knocked down by a carriage and run over. A traffic officer and some witnesses to the accident tried to arrest the driver. Kaka, seeing the scared look on his face, said to the officer: "Let him go free. It was my fault, for I am deaf and I didn't hear the carriage." As a result of this accident, Kaka became confined to his bed. Since his aged wife was unable to look after him in this state, his son, Dr. Ibrahim Sa'eed, took him to the city of Arak, where he was then practicing medicine, and cared for him until his death on March 7, 1940, at the age of eighty-five.

Reference has been made to Kaka's deafness. This was a serious handicap, especially in his later years, when he became practically stone-deaf. He rigged up a sort of homemade hearing aid, consisting of two bell-shaped amplifiers connected with a rubber tube a foot or so long. He would give one end to the person with whom he was talking to speak into and put the other end to his ear: this probably helped him somewhat. An American lady was once visiting in a missionary home when Kaka came along and the two were sitting on the porch. She knew no Persian but, supposing that Kaka knew English, began conversing with him in that language. Kaka could not hear a word she said but, thinking she was talking in Persian, tried to converse with her in his own tongue. Just what the substance of their conversation was is not recorded, but they seemed to get along famously. Kaka afterward remarked: "How strange it is that these missionaries come out from America and spend two or three years learning Persian, but this elderly lady has been in Iran only a few weeks and speaks it fluently!"

His deafness may have had the indirect benefit of preventing him from hearing some of the insults and curses hurled at him, and doubtless kept him from engaging in much useless argument, but it also made it increasingly difficult to carry on a religious conversation and so was a real hindrance to his work. However, it did not prevent him from presenting his Christian message to those who would listen.

No account of Kaka would be complete without some word of his family life. He did not marry until after he settled in Hamadan. The girl on whom he bestowed his affection bore the name of Hayat (meaning "life") and was the daughter of Muslim parents. She was fifteen or sixteen years of age at the time and a pupil in the American Girls' School in the city. Her marriage to a Christian aroused some of the fanatical Muslims of Hamadan and they protested to the governor, who put her father in jail, but he was soon released. Hayat Khanum* proved a capable wife and homemaker.

Just when she accepted the Christian faith it would be difficult to say. Probably it was a gradual process. One of her older children testifies that she had such a faith long before he knew what Christianity was and that he owes 80 percent of his own faith to her. She never made a public profession of her faith while living in Hamadan, presumably because of the dangers from bigoted Muslims in the early days. On the other hand, she read the Bible both in private and to her children and was a great believer in prayer, urging her children to pray. When some of her children were small, there was a narrow street between their home and the school through which two of them and the boys from the boarding school had to pass four times a day. At one place on this street was a wall built of mud, so old and cracked that it might fall at any time. Hayat Khanum was anxious for her chidren, lest it crash on them. So one night she gathered her children together and asked them to pray earnestly that the wall fall down in the middle of the night, when no one would be passing that way. The next morning they found the wall down. Mother and children gathered again to thank the Lord.

During her last years Hayat Khanum was confined to her bed at the home of Dr. Ibrahim, who had moved to Teheran after his father's death. The two of them often had conversation on spiritual things. One day he suggested to her that it would be well if she was baptized before she went to her heavenly home. She agreed and he hurried away to break the news to a missionary friend and arrange for the baptism. "Please come quickly to my home!" he said excitedly. "For fifty years I have prayed that my mother would be baptized, and at last she is ready." The ceremony was performed the next day for this lady of ninety years and her great-granddaughter of four. Several years later, in 1965, she passed away with the peace of a genuine faith in her Savior.

Kaka and Hayat Khanum had eight children, six boys and two girls. Discipline was left largely to their mother, but their father was very strict about certain things. For example, games with cards of any kind were definitely taboo. They were all regarded potentially dangerous, first steps on the road to gambling. With difficulty the children could have enough coins to buy a pack of cards to play a simple matching game, but once their father found them, they disappeared, never to

* Khanum is a polite term used in speaking of a woman, like Mrs. or Miss.

29

be seen again. Once or twice they outwitted him by making their own brand out of thick paper, but as soon as these were discovered, they went the way of those they had bought.

After the first World War, European novels, translated into Persian, found their way into the Iranian market. Like most of their friends, Kaka's children borrowed these books — works of Dumas, Victor Hugo, George Sand, Dostoievski, etc. When Kaka saw his children reading these books, he became suspicious. As he watched them eagerly devour one volume after another, he would express his disgust with a "Pah!" The children tried to hide their books among others on a shelf, but they would be discovered. However, since they came from a library, Kaka couldn't very well destroy them. Not having read them, Kaka became curious as to their nature, and once or twice, coming home unexpectedly, the children caught him reading one of these dangerous books. He would look up sheepishly with an embarrassed smile. They, in their turn, teased him by imitating his "Pah!", adding, "unworthy reading for a serious mind." After he came to discover the real nature of the books, he even read some of them aloud to the family in the evening.

Of his children, three became physicians and two of them teachers, one of whom later went to America and was for years connected with *The Voice of America*. One of the doctors, now practicing in the United States, wrote a biography of his uncle, Dr. Sa'eed,* which has been translated in whole or in part into five languages of the Middle and Far East. One grandson is a pillar of the Anglican Church in Isfahan.

Kaka, though a proud mulla when still a Muslim, became a man of great *humility*. If he spoke of himself, it was in terms of self-depreciation. He truly incarnated the teaching of Christ that His followers should become as little children. The blessing of the first Beatitude was assuredly his, for he was "poor in spirit." Along with his humility was a certain childlike *trustfulness*. Guileless himself, he was not suspicious of others. He took people for what they appeared to be and did not question their motives. One of his children declared that he could not remember ever hearing his father speak in an unkindly way of anyone.

Another trait that Kaka possessed is what we call *determination* in those whom we like and stubbornness in those we dislike. When he planned an itinerating trip, he would adhere strictly to that plan. A missionary lady with whom he frequently went on these tours, illustrates this characteristic by

* See footnote at the beginning of Chapter I.

the following typical conversation: "Kaka, this is the path to A . . . , where I wish especially to see two women." "No, we will not go there on this trip." "But I promised the women I would be there about this time." "No, we shall go to B . . . instead." And of course they did! Possibly it was because he felt that he had the leading of the Holy Spirit in the choices he made and hence he ought not to deviate. Once he had made the decision to accept the Christian faith, it was this same trait that made him adhere to it to the end without swerving, whatever the persecution involved.

Kaka was a man of deep and abiding *faith*. If he trusted his fellow men, he trusted God with greater certainty. After being run over by the carriage, he was bedridden for nearly two years till his death. In all this time there was no complaining or doubt of the divine Providence which had permitted this accident. During these days he told his son who was caring for him that when he was knocked down and run over, the weight of the carriage was so heavy and the pain so excruciating that at that very moment there flashed into his mind what a tremendous burden was the load of sin which Jesus voluntarily bore for the saving of mankind. With this thought he began to praise him for his gracious love in spite of his own suffering.

Along with this deep faith was a keen *evangelistic spirit*. Having accepted the Christian faith, he felt it a prime duty to propagate it. What meant so much to him must be shared with others. He delighted to tell the story of his own conversion and that of his brother and it made a deep impression. Once he was freed from other duties and appointed an evangelist, he gave himself wholeheartedly to this work. Neither curses nor threats could discourage him from distributing tracts in the streets. Evangelistic trips to the villages were the joy of his life. He looked forward eagerly to them, and when he thought it was time to take another, he would approach one of the missionaries with the request to be sent out. Even near the end of his life, when he was in his seventies, no longer strong and greatly handicapped by his deafness, he asked to be allowed to go on a trip. Refused by those in charge of the work, who thought it unwise because of his advanced age and inability to hear, he felt it a keen disappointment. He was at heart an evangelist.

Kaka's *devotional life* was one of his distinguishing features. It was his practice in the mornings to retire to a corner of the room, which was his private altar, or possibly to a separate room, for a time of quiet communion with God. In the evenings, he used to pray in a whisper after the light was out. One of his children testifies that, although they never had such a thing as family worship in the home, his father's never failing habit of quiet devotion was to him a source of inspiration in his later years. Kaka was a man of prayer and he often said to his children that no one could bear the burdens of life or meet its responsibilities, if he was a stranger to prayer. Those who traveled with him on his evangelistic trips might see him sitting up on his cot in the middle of the night and hear him praying; being deaf, he did not realize that his voice was more than a whisper. The sound was audible, but the words were indistinguishable. His prayers in public meetings, spoken with a touch of Kurdish pronunciation, were impressive and manifestly from his heart.

Kaka spent much time reading his Bible. It was his special companion. How many times he had read the Bible from cover to cover no one knows. One of his children writes to this effect: "One of the most priceless treasures that I have is his Bible. The pages are nearly worn out from continuous usage. Whenever I see the annotations in the margin and important passages underlined, I get a heart throb."

Kaka was a thoroughly dedicated Christian. Although he did not have the education or reputation of his doctor brother, his witness to his faith was just as sincere. The change in his life from a rabid Muslim fanatic, ready to murder his brother, to the humble, loving follower of Christ constitutes a convincing testimony to the truth and power of the Christian faith. His whole life might be summed up in the words with which he often signed his letters — "Kaka, the slave of Jesus Christ."

3

Sa'eed, the Physician

Let us now continue the story of Sa'eed, the younger of the two Kurdish brothers. At the end of Chapter I, we left him settled in Hamadan and acting as Dr. Alexander's interpreter and assistant. In this capacity he went with the doctor on a trip to Teheran, where he came down with a severe attack of dysentery. Confined to his bed, he had ample opportunity to meditate. He was disturbed by the recollection that at times in conversation with Muslims he had concealed his faith. He made a vow that, if he recovered, he would never again hesitate to confess his beliefs openly. He soon had a chance to prove the sincerity of his vow, for on his return home he was sent to Kermanshah, a city about 115 miles to the southwest, on an evangelistic trip with Kasha Shimmon, a pastor from Urumia serving in Hamadan. In Kermanshah he ran across many Kurds from Senneh and to them he testified to his new found faith. In the clinic in Hamadan he also met many a Kurd from his native district, to whom he read from the Bible or with whom he had discussion.

From these opportunities for evangelistic witness in the clinic, Sa'eed came to realize what a powerful influence medicine had to disarm prejudice and open the way for Christian evangelism. As a result, he decided to become a physician. Dr. Alexander gave his full approval and took him on as a medical student.

A new problem now presented itself. Sa'eed was tutoring Kasha Shimmon's children in their home. After some months he fell in love with Rebka (Syriac for Rebecca), one of the pastor's daughters. The affection was mutual. When Kasha Shimmon was approached on the subject of matrimony, he refused absolutely, both on the account of the different backgrounds and because of the danger to his family and the Christian community of such a union. When the Armenian community learned of the situation, they were indignant and

33

alarmed. They feared what the Muslims of the city might do, for such a union was contrary to all precedent. So they went to the missionaries and asked that Sa'eed be sent away from Hamadan. To avoid trouble they sent him to Teheran, when again he became sick.

In the spring of 1887, Dr. Alexander returned to Iran from a furlough in the United States and wanted Sa'eed's help in his clinic. So back he came, much to the anxiety of the Armenians. Again he asked Kasha Shimmon for leave to marry Rebka. The pastor finally agreed on one condition, that he be publicly baptized. Sa'eed was overjoyed, for this was the very thing for which he had been asking. So on April 10, 1887, the sacrament of baptism took place, Muslims as well as Christians being present. Kasha Shimmon now gave full approval to the marriage, but at once another obstacle arose: Mr. Hawkes refused to perform the ceremony, lest Sa'eed be killed as a result and Kasha Shimmon never cease to blame him. So a whole year passed until Kasha Yohanan visited Hamadan and agreed to tie the nuptial bond. A simple ceremony was held in the pastor's home in the presence of a few friends.

Now trouble arose. The Armenians, to defend themselves, broadcast news of the wedding, taking pains to explain that the bride was an Assyrian, not an Armenian. Consequently, the next day notices were posted around the city calling on faithful Muslims to avenge the enormity of this unholy marriage. A mob soon assembled and began marching through the streets and shouting. Dr. Alexander realized the need of speedy action. Fortunately, he had given medical attention to two of the most influential men of the city, the governor and one of the leading mullas. He at once went to see them and urged them to prevent any untoward happening. When the mob reached the governor's headquarters, he stepped out onto the balcony and claimed he had a letter from Sa'eed in which he denied that he became a Christian. With that he drew a letter from his pocket and pretended to read. The ruse worked. The people scattered. Another crowd that had gathered at the main mosque of the city was calmed by the mulla and dispersed. And so the young couple were left undisturbed in their married joy, though the bride for some time lived in great fear for her husband.

During these days Sa'eed was working hard at his medical studies and making good progress. From time to time he made trips to neighboring villages and wherever he went he witnessed to his faith. When his contract with the Mission terminated in 1891, he made a trip to Urumia, where Rebka had already gone with their first child, a little girl. On his return to Hamadan, Sa'eed was requested to renew his contract with the Mis-

sion. Though hesitant to do so, he consented to carry on for a
year, since the Mission had been obliged to close the clinic because of Dr. Alexander's resignation and they were waiting for
someone to succeed him. His responsibilities were heavy, and
made heavier by an outbreak of cholera. Sa'eed was near a
breakdown, but he carried on till the spring, when the new
doctor arrived, and then turned in his resignation. This was in
1893.

Sa'eed now determined to make a trip to Europe. He felt it
advisable to have a change of climate to build up his health and
he also wanted further medical training. He went first to Sweden
and then to London, where he was introduced to Dr. and Mrs.
C. E. H. Warren, who took him into their home, where he
lived for two years. Dr. Warren guided him in choosing his
medical course and they introduced him to the Plymouth
Brethren, a religious group without formal organization, to
which they belonged. In this group he found warm fellowship
and spiritual uplift. He himself finally joined it. As for his
medical studies, he took courses in anatomy, physiology, opthalmology and tropical diseases. On his return home he had been
away for two years and a half.

Dr. Sa'eed now set up practice on his own in Hamadan. With
the help of friends in England, he was able to buy a house for
his family. His work demanded seeing patients at all hours of
the day, whenever it suited them to call.

These were days of uncertainty and disorder for everybody.
Naser-ed-Din Shah was assassinated in May, 1896. Hamadan
was upset by a struggle between two parties of mullas over a
religious question. At night bullets whizzed through the air.
There was looting and killing. It was an especially difficult time
for a Muslim convert to witness to his faith, but the doctor kept
at it.

At the turn of the century he was called by the son-in-law of
the Shah, who was also governor of several provinces in the
southwest of Iran, to attend his wife. For a whole year he served
this prince and his retinue of five thousand during an inspection
trip he was making of the area under his control. After com-
pletion of this undertaking, he was called upon to render service
in the royal household. This he performed so satisfactorily that
Mozaffar-ed-Din Shah wished to retain him as Court Physician.
Dr. Sa'eed, however, did not wish to expend his skill and talents
on a few privileged people, but to use his abilities for all who
needed them. To show his appreciation, the Shah conferred
a title on Sa'eed, a title which he never used and which most
people did not know that he had.

In the winter of 1901 he made another trip to Urumia, but

the storms were so severe and the snow so deep in places that it took nearly three months, including stops along the road for rest. Sometimes he had to stay in a village home and when they found he was a Christian, they felt their home defiled, but no such objection was raised against the money he paid for his entertainment or the medical service he rendered.

In Urumia he was everywhere cordially welcomed. His father-in-law, Kasha Shimmon, was delighted to entertain him. He spent four months there, giving himself to personal evangelism rather than public preaching. At the end of this period, he decided he must return, in spite of reports that reached him of danger that had arisen in Hamadan. Upon request he had given a mulla there a copy of *The Sources of Islam,* a book written by an English missionary to show what elements in Islam had come from the Old Testament, from Christian heretical books, from Zoroastrianism, etc., whereas the Muslim belief is that the Koran had descended from God himself. The book had let loose a storm of anger. It was claimed that Dr. Sa'eed had written it and the leading ecclesiastic in Hamadan had decreed his death. In spite of this, Sa'eed felt he must return. He was accompanied part way by his brother-in-law, Dr. Jesse Yonan, just back from hospital training in the United States, who was planning to go as a medical evangelist to Kurdistan.

They had been warned not to go through the town of Sauj-bulagh (now Mahabad), for it was reported that two men had come there from Sanadaj on an errand of evil. They discussed what road to take. Finally, Dr. Sa'eed pointed out that they had been urging the Assyrians along the way to trust in God. Why, then, should they fear to go through Saujbulagh? So ahead they went. As they neared the town, they were met by envoys from the Governor of the province urging them to be his guests. They expressed their gratitude, but asked to be excused. However, they accepted an invitation to dinner the next day. A group of mullas present wanted to hear from Dr. Sa'eed himself why he had turned away from Islam. So a meeting was arranged for the following day, at which Sa'eed answered their questions without hesitation. At the close the two men from Sanandaj against whom the doctor had been warned, came forward, but they proved to be old classmates of his who greeted him warmly. When the two doctors left the city the next day, about two hundred people gathered to see them off.

A few days later the two men separated, each to go his own way. Sa'eed reached home without incident and rejoiced to be united with his family again after an absence of more than six months.

In spite of all the prejudice stirred up against Dr. Sa'eed in his absence, he now settled down to a successful practice with little disturbance. After about a year (1902) he decided to make another trip to England to put his older son, Samuel,* in school there and also to take further studies, this time in typology, bacteriology, opthalmology, and eye surgery. As a result of this further training, upon his return to Hamadan the following year he performed some brilliant cures, which enhanced his reputation and deepened the jealousy of local doctors. Among these patients who were healed was the little son of the governor of the province, who was the brother of the Shah.

In the summer of 1904 a severe epidemic of cholera broke out in Hamadan. Well-to-do people fled the city. The governor with his family and retinue set up a camp on a tableland six thousand feet above the city and here he summoned Dr. Sa'eed to serve as their physician. Jealous of the governor's power was a wealthy landowner, Amir Afkham, who lived in the village of Shavarin about four miles outside the city. It happened that his wife and daughter were critically ill. When they became worse, he humbled himself by asking the governor to release Sa'eed, in order to treat his two sick ladies. The doctor was able to cure both, greatly to the joy of the Amir.

With the coming of cold weather the epidemic came to an end and people who had fled returned to their homes. And now new trouble arose for Sa'eed. Some Jewish doctors who had left their faith for Bahaism, jealous of his successes, gave a copy of *The Sources of Islam* to some fanatical mullas, claiming it was written by Sa'eed. The Amir was hoping that this would create a disturbance which the governor would be unable to quell and hence he would have to resign. The mullas gathered in the central mosque and signed a decree ordering Sa'eed's death for writing a book that blasphemed their Prophet and for trying to seduce Muslims to apostatize. If read in public, this decree would be a call to the faithful to rise up and carry it out.

The governor was unable to do anything, but by telegram informed the Prime Minister of what was happening. The Amir sought to quiet things down, but it had gone too far, so he sent an escort to bring Sa'eed to Shavarin, where he arrived at night. When it became known where he was, a band of fanatics with hired assassins set out for the village. They were

* A second son, Lemuel, had been born in 1896, completing his family of three children.

headed off with great difficulty by two mullas, who swore by their Prophet that Sa'eed had already left the place.

The Amir now told Sa'eed that he could no longer provide him refuge and showed him a telegram from the Prime Minister telling him to send the doctor at once to Teheran. So Sa'eed left for the capital, where he learned that the whole affair was an intrigue by which the Amir wanted to get the governor out of Hamadan. The mullas were only instruments in the plot, and Sa'eed was the victim.

Sa'eed now wanted his wife to sell their property and come to Teheran, but Rebka preferred Hamadan. Finally, they compromised: she would go to Teheran, but they would keep the property.

After about seven years of practicing medicine in the capital, Dr. Sa'eed in 1912 returned to Hamadan to take up his residence and resume his practice there. Before long a request came for his services in a village on the border of Kurdistan from a landowner famed for his beautiful handwriting. The doctor went, escorted by six armed riders sent to accompany him. He found the patient suffering from mental decline resulting from brain inflammation. Sa'eed was able to effect such a great improvement in a short time that the landowner's sons said he read and wrote as well as he had done twenty years before.

While he was still in this village, a letter came to him from Sayyid* Najm-ed-Din, an important personage who had followers from the Caspian basin across Iran to its western border. It was a request to come to his village in Kurdistan to treat a relative. Sa'eed and his friends thought it unwise for him to go to such a fanatical district, so he replied asking to be excused. His letter accidentally fell into a fire when the messenger was drying his clothes on the way back. After a week another letter came from the same man, which made it clear that the person who wanted his help was the Sultan of Awraman, near the Turkish border, a district from which Sa'eed's family had come. What should he do? He couldn't refuse the blind Sultan of his own people, and yet to go there was to imperil his life. Some one suggested he ask the Sultan for an enormous fee and perchance that would end the matter; so he replied that he would come for fifty tomans (about $50) a day, a huge fee for that time. In due season Sayyid Jalal-ed-Din, the son of Sayyid Najm-ed-Din, arrived with a large escort and a promise to pay whatever the doctor should ask.

The very next day came a letter from Sanandaj from the governor of the province, together with letters from some of the

* A sayyid is a descendant of Mohammed.

38

dignitaries of the city, begging the doctor to come to treat him. Here were requests from two very important men — men at odds with each other and both from fanatical places. After reflection and prayer, Sa'eed resolved to attempt both, with a written promise from Sayyid Jalal-ed-Din to escort him all the way on the return trip.

He decided to go first to Sanandaj, though the Sultan's men offered him 300 tomans not to go. He told them that his word of honor was worth more than any amount of money, so he proceeded to Sanandaj with the governor's escort. We can imagine his feelings as he entered the city he had left thirty years before, with all of its familiar spots and the memories of many experiences! All along through the streets he was greeted with shouts of welcome, instead of the curses of the old days.

The doctor found the governor suffering from chronic nephritis and high blood pressure. He gave an injection and ordered a hot bath. The next day he was much better. In the morning patients began to arrive and he treated them all without charge. After five days the governor had greatly improved, so he felt free to leave.

The journey to Awraman was not a long one, but very difficult — mountain paths so narrow that if the animal slipped, both rider and mount would be plunged over the edge hundreds of feet below. At one place the passage looked so dangerous that Sa'eed crossed on his hands and feet. The entrance to the Sultan's palace had been carpeted with a roll of calico and at the end was a beautiful rug on which the Sultan awaited his guest. He embraced Sa'eed, kissing him on both cheeks according to Iranian custom.

An examination of the Sultan's eyes was discouraging in the extreme. Both were afflicted with trachoma; the left eye had been operated on by an incapable oculist and suffered from glaucoma, which produced severe headaches. Furthermore, he was diabetic. In fact, an operation failed to give the least prospect of success. So Sa'eed sent word to the Sultan that his case was hopeless and asked for permission to leave. The Sultan pleaded with him: "I will give everything I have. Only let me see through the eye that has not been operated on." But the doctor could only reply that the operation would be dangerous and might increase the pain and headache and at the same time ruin his own reputation. The Sultan could only accept the verdict. It was arranged that Sa'eed should leave the next morning.

That night the passage for Sa'eed's Bible reading was the story of Lazarus. As he read, it was as if he could hear God speaking to him: "Jesus hears that his friend is critically ill. In spite of danger he goes to minister to him because he knows it is his Father's will. Have I not guided you every step of the way on this journey? I have kept you from all harm. I have sent you to this old man who has been pleading for four years, 'Send me Sa'eed to heal my eyes.' But you are abandoning him, trusting in your own knowledge rather than in me, with whom all things are possible." Sa'eed answered, "I obey, leaving the outcome to Thee."

In the morning he told Jalal-ed-Din to report to the Sultan that he had changed his decision and would attempt the operation, and to ask for a messenger to take a telegram to Sanandaj, to be sent to Hamadan for his instruments. The Sultan was overjoyed.

Although it would be at least a week before the instruments could arrive, the doctor began preparations for the operation. He put the patient on a strict diet to improve his general condition. He had the mud floor of the room chosen for the operation covered with calico to prevent footsteps stirring up dust. The same was done with the ceiling to prevent particles of dirt from dropping. In the meantime, from early morning he was treating patients for all sorts of diseases. In addition, many of his relatives came to call on him.

The surgical instruments finally arrived from Hamadan. The day was set for the operation. It was November and the days were short. It was late when they started. The conjunctiva was ruined. The cornea had become a horny mass which the doctor could only cut with difficulty. The iris fell to pieces. He finally cut the lens loose and removed it. He was relieved to find the Sultan could count his fingers. He finally shut the eye, bandaged it, and gave instructions that it should be kept closed for four days. Sa'eed testified that he had had no faith in his own skill, but in God.

When the four days were up, the doctor removed the bandages and asked the Sultan if he could see anything. He said he could. Just at that moment his daughter quietly came into the room. Sa'eed asked him who it was. He replied that it was she. All three were greatly moved. The doctor covered the eye and repeated his translation of the hymn written by Joseph Hart in 1450:

> How good is the God we adore;
> Our faithful, unchangeable friend,
> Whose love is as great as his power,
> And knows neither measure nor end!

The Sultan was greatly impressed and asked Sa'eed to operate on his wife's eyes. When he had finished with one eye, she said that she could see so well with it she would not trouble him to do the other.

The day come for Sa'eed to leave. The Sultan gave him an escort of fifty men, twenty on horseback, thirty walking. At last they reached Sanandaj. On every hand people congratulated him, for during his absence all sorts of rumors had been rife. After a few days of rest he was ready to depart for Hamadan. Jalal-ed-Din came to say goodbye with tears in his eyes. He said: "All the time during this trip I have been thinking of the time I should return to my home. Now that it is here, I am sad. You have made me see the light, and for the help you have given me I pray God to bless you."

It was only a day or two before Christmas when Sa'eed reached home, a time of rejoicing for him and his family! He praised God for having kept him through all the dangers of the journey, for enabling him to heal so many patients, and for giving him the opportunity to witness in his homeland of Kurdistan.

In 1913, the following year, he made his third trip to England. His two sons were there. Samuel had been there eleven years and was now studying engineering. Lemuel had been there about seven years and needed another year to finish his general education. Dr. Sa'eed was anxious to see his sons and he himself needed a change after his many years of arduous practice. The opportunity to go to Europe came through the chance to accompany a patient there. His stay in London enabled him to take some advanced work in two hospitals where he had studied before. It also made possible a visit to Sir William Osler, the world-renowned physician, with whom he had had correspondence regarding the tomb of Avicenna, a famous Persian doctor of the eleventh century who was buried in Hamadan. Dr. Osler was greatly interested in erecting a suitable tomb that would serve as a memorial for this celebrated physician and philosopher. He had enlisted Dr. Sa'eed's help, but before Dr. Osler's appeal could bear much fruit, the First World War erupted and delayed everything. Shortly after the conclusion of the war, Dr. Osler died and the whole matter was held up. With the money raised, a building was erected in which there was a reading room. Later on the Iranian Ministry of Education took up the project. Plans were drawn for an elaborate mausoleum and library. The structure was dedicated in 1954 in the presence of the King and Queen and distinguished orientalists.

On his return from England, Dr. Sa'eed resumed his practice in Hamadan. Soon World War I broke out. In the summer of 1916 the Turkish army came up to Hamadan from Baghdad and the Christian community, mostly Armenians, left the city before their arrival. Among them were Sa'eed and his family. Rebka, with her independent spirit, stayed on and Lemuel, who had returned from England and was in Teheran, came to stay with her. The Turks, unable to get hold of the "apostate," destroyed hundreds of dollars worth of trees on his country place outside the city, giving as their excuse that Sa'eed had treated Russian soldiers when they occupied the city and that his son Samuel was serving in the British army. The British government later offered an indemnity, but he declined it.

Dr. Sa'eed was now settled in Teheran, which was his residence for the remainder of his days. His life was quiet with the busy routine of his medical work. His home and clinic adjoined each other near the center of the city, across the street from the Ministry of War and the American Presbyterian Mission. He rose early, had his time of private devotions, followed by breakfast, and was in his well-attended clinic from half-past eight till noon and again from two o'clock till dark, except when he went out for house calls. He was thorough in examining patients, but never wrote down case histories, relying on his retentive memory. Twice a week he held Bible readings in his home — on Sundays especially for Christians and on Thursdays for Muslims and any others who wished to attend. Rebka had joined him and ran the household with efficiency.

As the years went by and Sa'eed passed his seventieth birthday, he gradually slowed down in his practice. While vacationing at his summer place in Hamadan, a call came from Sanandaj to treat the governor's wife. It was a brief trip, on which he was accompanied by his son-in-law, Dr. Tatevos, and Kaka, as narrated in Chapter II.

Two years later, when again summering in Hamadan, Dr. Sa'eed was summoned one day to the police office. He was told it was to see a patient, but since he was escorted by two policemen, he realized he was under arrest. He couldn't imagine why. When he was interrogated by an officer, he found that it was because of a letter of condolence he had written to the daughter of a Kurdish chief who had been his patient and who had recently died. This man, along with others, had been held as a hostage in Teheran by Reza Shah, father of the present King, in his efforts to bring certain tribes under control. In the course of his letter to Dr. Sa'eed had written: "You must be glad that he died in his home, surrounded by his family — not like Sowlat-ud-Dowleh (the title of the head of the Kashgai tribe), Taimur-tash (former Minister of the court) and others, some of whom were taken through the country and died in prison." Although the fate of the two men mentioned was a well-known fact, the officer asked Dr. Sa'eed how he knew they had died in prison and charged him with being closely connected with them. With that he summoned a policeman to take him to a room in the jail — a room with only a wooden bedstead and a few bedclothes of questionable character. That night he had little sleep. The next day Dr. Tatevos was allowed to bring him a cot and food from home. For two months and a half he was confined here while the officials in Hamadan waited for instructions from Teheran. His family and friends were allowed to visit him. During this time he had many letters of sympathy, some from the most influential people in Kurdistan, even religious leaders. They had to write in guarded language, of course, but the sympathy of such men, who had formerly sought his life, was a source of great cheer in these dark days.

After two months and a half, he was sent to Teheran under guard. Here his friends were working for his release, but in vain. Samuel even went twice to see the Prime Minister, whom the doctor had at one time cured when other physicians failed, but he intimated that he was helpless. Only Reza Shah could order his release. Finally, Samuel wrote a long telegram to the Shah, saying that the letter his father had written had been misinterpreted, and requesting that he be pardoned. This method proved effective and Dr. Sa'eed's release was ordered. It was a time of great rejoicing for family and friends. Letters of congratulations came from every quarter. His imprisonment had lasted ninety-nine days. He said it was the best rest he had had in fifty years!

The following year Dr. Sa'eed moved into a new house built for him by his engineer son, Samuel. It was a three-story brick building — two floors and a basement, all arranged for his comfort. Here he hoped to have more time for reading, writing, and study. The sign that had been over his clinic was no longer in evidence, but still some of his patients were persistent in seeking him out and he did not have the heart to refuse them. However, he found more time for his studies.

Hardly a year had passed in this new house when Rebka was taken ill. She lingered on for months and finally passed away in November, 1939. Her death brought deep heartache to her companion of more than fifty years. The funeral, held in the mission church, was attended by hundreds of people from Cabinet Ministers to the poor whom she had helped.

Less than four months later came the news of Kaka's death to add to Sa'eed's sorrow. The reports of the Second World War cast a gloom over everything. Samuel, who was giving up his work, was planning to retire in America to be with his wife and children. A final family reunion was held on Sa'eed's seventy-ninth birthday, June 1, 1942. Three days later Samuel departed for the United States and his father left for Hamadan for his annual outing there.

Not two months had passed when on July 29, in the quiet of his garden, he was taken ill with a heart attack and died the same day. The funeral, which took place in the beautiful chapel which Mr. Hawkes had built in memory of his wife, was attended by a great crowd of people of many nationalities. One of his own hymns was sung, a hymn that pays tribute to the perfections of Christ. He was buried in the Protestant cemetery next to the graves of his lifelong friends, Mr. and Mrs. Hawkes. On his tombstone are the words, "For I am not ashamed of the Gospel of Christ, for it is the power of God to everyone that believeth" (Romans 1:16). Let us take a look at some of Dr. Sa'eed's traits of character, among the many that might be noted.

First, *his search for truth*. In his early days, while still a Muslim, he studied his Koran. He read Islamic law and learned Mohammedan traditions. When Kasha Yohanan came to Sanandaj, he began to study the Bible. Not only did he ask the Christian evangelist the meaning of this verse and that passage, but he took up the study of both ancient and modern Syriac, and Hebrew as well, in order to compare translations and the better to understand meanings. He examined carefully the prophecies of the Old Testament to see how they were fulfilled in the life of Christ. At the height of his uncertainty, as he wavered between Islam and Christianity, he prayed in a passion of fervor: "O Guide of Wanderers, lead me in the true way which is according to thy will. Take away the veil and give comfort to my heart." Not long afterward his prayer was answered. When Mar Shimmon, a Catholic bishop of note who was well-versed in the Bible, came to Sanandaj, Sa'eed took occasion to visit him often during his short stay there to delve further into the Scriptures under his guidance.

His first trip to Europe was in pursuit of two kinds of truth—spiritual truth and medical knowledge. He had met a Swedish missionary in Hamadan who claimed he had attained spiritual perfection. If that was possible, he was determined to find it. So his stay in Sweden was planned for this purpose, but through further acquaintance with the missionary and his colleagues, he failed to obtain this objective. It was only when a verse from the New Testament flashed into his mind at the time of his morning devotions that he realized that perfections were not for this life: "We know that, *when he shall appear*, we shall be like him" (I John 3:2).

His eager pursuit of medical knowledge began in his early

days in Hamadan. While working with Dr. Alexander, he often stayed up till after midnight poring over the works of Razi and Avicenna, two ancient Persian physicians of great fame. In London he studied assiduously for two years to obtain still further knowledge. On a later trip he again undertook study. His thirst for truth was never slaked.

Nor was it only in the fields of medicine and Christian faith that Dr. Sa'eed was ever seeking for knowledge. Being a Kurd, he was deeply interested in the Ahl-i-Haqq, or Ali-Ullahis, a heretical sect of Muslims found in Kurdistan, and he read a scholarly paper on this strange religion at the Inter-Mission Conference in Teheran in 1926. Also, he had an intimate knowledge of the Babi-Baha'i Movement. Some of the early Babis, including the widow of the Bab, were his patients and friends, and he had a valuable collection of rare, handwritten Babi books, which are now in the Princeton University Library. He found nothing in these religions which could compare with the treasures he had found in Christ.

Dr. Sa'eed was a deeply *spiritual man*. While yet a Muslim he sought close relation to God. As a young boy, long before he was required to perform the Islamic rites, he began attending public prayers at the mosque. Later on, during the month of Ramazan, the Muslim month of fasting, he practiced special devotional exercises: nightly he sang special prayers from the rooftop. While others spent the night in feasting, he allowed himself just one meal in the evening and a sip of water at dawn before the day's fasting began. In order to perfect his spiritual life, he sought membership in the mystic order of Naqshbandis, a widespread sect of dervishes. He had heard that some of these men fasted forty days and thereafter had marvelous visions. So he was initiated into this order and for three years he practiced their rites faithfully night after night.

As a Christian he was an ardent student of the Bible. It was his closest companion. On his flight to Hamadan, when Kaka returned to take him back to Sanandaj and Sa'eed refused to go, Kaka took his bag that contained his cherished books and started off, hoping this artifice would induce his brother to follow him. Sa'eed cried out, "Take everything, but give me back my Bible!" The same spirit held all through his life. When he rose in the morning, he would not start the day without reading from it, nor did he lie down at night without a further look into it. When he called on patients, he took it with him, and often read to them from it. The margins of his Bible were covered with his notes. It was his meat and drink, his guide in daily life, his consolation in trouble.

Along with his study of the Bible went prayer — prayer that

45

was real communion with God. How sorry he was for Iranian Muslims, who said their prayers by rote in Arabic, a language they did not understand! He prayed for his family. He prayed for his patients. When faced with a difficult decision, he sought the guidance of God, and oftentimes it came to him when he was on his knees. When confronted with a formidable task, he invariably asked God's help. And when the task was successfully completed, he poured out his thanksgiving to the One who had helped him.

Dr. Sa'eed's spiritual life was centered in Christ, and Christ was everything to him. Of the hymns which he wrote, the one most often sung in the churches, and the one which best reveals his own mind and heart, has been translated from Persian as follows:

> Christ is my Life, and Christ is my Light;
> Christ is my Guide in the darkness of night;
> Priest and strong Advocate Christ is for me;
> Christ is my Master, to truth He's the key.
>
> Christ is my Leader, He peace to me brought;
> Christ is my Savior, Christ righteousness wrought;
> Christ is my Prophet, my Priest, and my King;
> My Way, and the Truth to which firmly I cling.
>
> Christ is my Glory, and Christ is my Crown;
> Christ shares my troubles when woe strikes me down;
> Christ is my Treasure in heaven above;
> In every deep sorrow he soothes me with love.
>
> Christ is my Savior, my Portion, my Lord;
> All honor and homage to Him I accord.
> Christ is my Peace, and Christ my Repast;
> Christ is my Rapture forever to last.
>
> In joy and in sorrow Christ satisfies me;
> 'Tis Christ who from bondage of sin set me free.
> In all times of sickness Christ is my Health;
> In want and in poverty Christ is my Wealth.

A third characteristic of Dr. Sa'eed was his *evangelistic spirit.* There have been many Muslims who in their hearts accepted the Christian faith, but who feared to make confession of it because of persecution or ostracism that might follow, but not Dr. Sa'eed. He was not only ready to confess his belief, but sought opportunity to do so and urged others to accept it. He talked with his patients about his faith and what it meant to him. To heal the body was not enough; the soul must be healed as well. When summoned before the authorities, he never denied his beliefs to save himself. It made no difference whether he was being entertained in a village home on a journey or whether he was the guest of the governor of a province, he gave his witness boldly.

Courage was another trait that Sa'eed possessed in abundance, as has been made clear in the preceding pages. One day in the year 1912 two missionaries in Teheran were discussing the question as to whether the time had come when a Muslim convert should be asked to preach in the Sunday service in the mission chapel, to which numerous Muslims came. As they were talking Dr. Sa'eed passed by. "Yes," said Dr. Samuel Jordan to his colleague, "the time has come, and there is the preacher!" Dr. Sa'eed was consulted, and he replied that he must first consult his Lord. The next day he agreed to preach, and the sermon which he delivered in the service was on the cleansing of Naaman the Syrian, which he later published as a widely-circulated tract. There were no serious consequences of Dr. Sa'eed's bold act, and this set a precedent for other converts to occupy the pulpit.

Of other traits of Dr. Sa'eed that might be mentioned, let us consider just one — his *loving treatment of his enemies*. Whenever he had a chance to do a kindness or give medical care to one who had injured him or who had tried to do him harm, he was always ready to do so. Consider testimonies such as these:

A leading mulla of Hamadan was one of the chief men who conspired to kill Sa'eed in 1904 and forced him to give up his practice in that city and flee to Teheran. A few years later when the doctor returned to Hamadan for a summer's rest, the mulla was very sick with a stomach ulcer. He sent for Sa'eed, who treated him free of charge with all kindness and skill and restored him to health. Whenever he or his family needed medical treatment, the procedure was always the same. On one occasion another mulla accompanied him to the doctor's office. To this friend he remarked: "I feel ashamed before the doctor. I have done him a great deal of evil, but he has always requited it with kindness. Once he even saved my life." On another occasion he remarked to a Christian physician: "I have done everything I could to end his life. In spite of that he always shows me kindness."

In the year 1911, when the government was under the rule of a regent, Salar-ud-Dowleh, brother of the Shah who had been deposed, gathered an army of tribesmen, many of whom were from Sanandaj and its neighborhood. He marched on the capital to occupy it, but was defeated. Captives from his army were taken to Teheran and put in prison, among them men who had vowed to kill Sa'eed. When Sa'eed returned to the capital from his summer vacation in Hamadan, he visited many of these prisoners, treated those who were wounded, and to some gave financial help. He was able to effect the release of many, whom he sent back to Kurdistan. The testimony of one is typical: "I was one of those who swore to kill him, but he healed my eyes, gave me money and clothing, and sent me home!"

One afternoon years later Dr. Sa'eed was conducting a meeting in his home for the study of the Bible, when an officer in a captain's uniform entered the room. He was plainly suffering pain from an abscess on his neck. The doctor asked him to wait till the Bible reading was over. After the meeting Sa'eed went to his dispensary to sterilize a scalpel. While he was gone, the captain said to the group: "You don't know me. Years ago I sought to kill the doctor, but this is the way he has treated me and my family ever since." After he had left, the others requested an explanation of the captain's remarks. The doctor said: "This man I have just treated is Mahmud Khan,* at one time a notorious bandit in Kurdistan. On my way back to Sanandaj from Awraman, he was hired to intercept our caravan and kill me, but Providence had my route changed and I was saved." For a year and a half Mahmud Khan and his family of twenty-five were under house arrest in Teheran and all this time Dr. Sa'eed treated them free of charge. He was faithful to the teaching of his Master: "Love your enemies, do good to those who hate you, bless them that curse you, and pray for those who despitefully use you" (Luke 6:27, 28).

It was because of such characteristics and because of all the generous and skillful service rendered to so many people that Sir Mortimer Durand, one-time British Minister to Iran, offered this testimony: "If in all the years of its activities the American Mission had achieved nothing more than the conversion of Dr. Sa'eed, then its labors had been amply repaid."

* Khan was formerly used as a polite term, like Mr., in speaking of a man.

4

The Martyr of Tabriz

To those who wanted to become his disciples, Jesus Christ said, "If any man would come after me, let him deny himself and take up his cross and follow me" (Matt. 16:24). In Muslim lands "taking up the cross" is more than a figure of speech. Only God knows the number of those converts to Christianity who since the rise of Islam have loved Christ more than life, and have joined the "noble army of martyrs." One of those who in Iran were faithful unto death was Mirza Ibrahim,* who died confessing Christ in Tabriz on May 14, 1893.

As a result of the work of American Presbyterian missionaries and Iranian evangelists, a number of Armenians who lived in the town of Khoi in northwestern Iran, near the borders of Turkey and Russia, became members of the Protestant church. In the year 1888 a Muslim man by the name of Ibrahim (Abraham) began to attend the meetings of these Christians, and to receive Christian instruction. As he came to understand more perfectly the pure Christianity which he found in this little meeting room, he became convinced of its truth, and he sought to be baptized as a Christian. The Christians, however, questioned his motives and he was delayed. But nothing discouraged him. His wife and friends scoffed at him but he stood firm, and after a year's probation he was openly received and baptized into the name of Christ. Believers and unbelievers were present, and saw with wonder the bold confession. One of those present was a Muslim, himself a half-believer, who after the ceremony gave Mirza Ibrahim the right hand of congratulation, wishing that he had like courage to avow his belief in Jesus.

* This biographical sketch has been taken chiefly from *Young Men Who Overcame* by Robert E. Speer (Revell, 1905), pp. 155-164. Speer quotes at length from "a sketch of Mirza Ibrahim" written by Dr. Benjamin Labaree, missionary in Urumia 1860-1906, whose son Benjamin, also a missionary, was murdered by Muslims near Khoi in 1904. This material has been used with the kind permission of Revell. Mirza, like Khan, is a polite term formerly used for men.

The test of his faith came immediately. His wife and children and small property were taken from him by fanatical Muslims, and though sick and feeble he was forced to flee. He went to Urumia, now called Rezaieh, and found refuge in the Presbyterian Mission Hospital, of which the famous Dr. Joseph Cochran, Sr., was the founder and superintendent, and there he found safety. In Urumia the simplicity and firmness of Ibrahim's faith won the confidence of all. He was first employed to copy books for a little Turkish-speaking school. Then, after a year or two, he was sent out at his own request to carry the Gospel to the villagers around, with the small compensation of four dollars a month.

With such fearlessness and vigor did he proclaim the way of life through Christ alone, that the wrath of the enemy was aroused against him. But he only grew the bolder. Such a course, however, could issue in but one way. The arm of the civil law, at the behest of Muslim ecclesiastics, was laid upon him. He was arrested and brought before the Sarparest, a sub-governor appointed over the Assyrian Christians in Urumia. When arraigned for investigation, with a crowd of scowling mullas and other Muslims gathered around, the Sarparest inquired of him, "Why should you, a Muslim, be teaching the Christian doctrines?"

 Mirza Ibrahim took out his New Testament from his bosom, and asked in reply, "Is not this Injil (Gospel) a holy book?" The Sarparest acknowledged that it was, for the Muslims believe that the Injil was given to Jesus by God. So the prisoner replied, "Am I not right then in reading it and teaching it?"

"But how about Mohammed?" was the question that followed. To this the prisoner replied, "That is for you to say; my faith is in Christ and his word; he is my Savior." At this the command was given to beat him, and Ibrahim was knocked down and terribly kicked, even by the Sarparest himself. Some in the crowd demanded his blood, but he was taken from this lower tribunal to the governor of the city, where, in the presence of many dignitaries, he reaffirmed his faith in Christ as the only Savior of his soul. Wealthy Muslim officials stood ready to raise a purse of money for him if the want of that had tempted him to abjure his allegiance to Islam. But his patient endurance of the abusive treatment heaped upon him proved to them that something other than money was at the bottom of his boldness. Some declared him crazy; but not a few of the military men, who had come to hold more liberal sentiments toward Christianity through their association with Dr. Cochran and the better class of Assyrian Christians, were convinced that Mirza Ibrahim had come to be an honest believer in Jesus Christ, and his courage in confessing him moved them much.

He was then thrown into prison with a chain about his neck, and his feet made fast in stocks and there he remained for three weeks. The city was in an uproar, and the mob about the prison gates demanded his execution. Torture and death stared him in the face as among the possibilities, but it was said that through all this ordeal his face shone like that of an angel, as did the face of Stephen, the first Christian martyr. Firmly he declared, "You may shoot me from the mouth of a cannon, but you cannot take away the salvation which Christ gave me."

In consequence of the uproar in the community and the desire of the authorities to avoid a violent termination of the case, it was decided to send Mirza Ibrahim to Tabriz, to appear before the highest tribunal of the province. An Assyrian Christian brother, who had been closely associated with Mirza Ibrahim in preaching Christ in the Muslim villages, went to bid him goodbye on the day he was to start for Tabriz. He found him tying his clothing in a handkerchief, ready to go. Turning to his fellow prisoners, Ibrahim said, "I have shown to you Christ, the all-sufficient Savior, and you have learned truth enough to save your souls, if you only receive it." Then he bade them a tender farewell. They all arose with heavy fetters on hands and feet and chains upon their necks, and bade him go in peace, as tears streamed down many of their wretched faces. His Christian friends had sent him an extra supply of provisions and the soldiers suggested that he take this with him for his journey's need. But he answered, "No, I have a Master who will provide for me; I will leave this bread for the poor prisoners here." As he left the prison he turned, and raising his right hand, solemnly called God to witness that if on the judgment day he should meet any of these souls unsaved, he had declared to them the way of life, and that he was free from their blood.

Eight soldiers took him to the house of the general commanding the cavalry, whose men were to escort him to Tabriz. A crowd of Muslims had gathered in the house, curious to see the man who dared to defy the mullas, and to deny the authority of their prophet. The mullas began plying him with questions and scoffing at him, but he answered them so clearly and pointedly that they became ashamed to pursue the matter before the assembled crowd. The general then permitted his Assyrian brother Absalom to have a final interview with the prisoner. They embraced one another affectionately, and spoke of faith and love, and possible death for the Master's sake.

To the missionaries and other friends he sent a message, asking that they pray to God for the increase of his faith. "Tell them," he said, "this firmness is not of myself, but God is helping me." They knelt together, the general and the mullas looking on, and each offered to God a parting prayer.

As they arose the general kindly said, "My son, have you finished?" After this Mirza Ibrahim was led out to mount the horse which friends had provided for his five days' journey; otherwise he must have gone on foot. The general was one of those who had been deeply impressed with the sincerity of the prisoner's new faith, and was ready to show him all the favor consistent with his position. To the escort of soldiers he said, "I swear by the spirit of Christ, if any of you maltreat this man, I will cause you to eat your fathers!"— a caustic form of threat. Ibrahim's last words to Absalom were, "Pray for me, that I may witness for Christ among my people. It is a privilege given to me, which perhaps may not be given to you Assyrians. Pray that I may be firm. I have no fear whatever, though I know I may have to die. Goodbye." As he went away a Muslim officer said, "This is a wonderful man; he is as brave as a lion!"

When Mirza Ibrahim reached Tabriz he was taken before the governor of the province, who was the Crown Prince, and was asked what had been given to him to induce him to become a Christian. His reply was, "Nothing but these bonds and this imprisonment." He was cast into a dark dungeon, his feet put in stocks, he was beaten and stoned, and a heavy iron collar and chain were fastened on his neck. At that time the Iranian government did not furnish prisoners with food, and unless friends helped them they would starve. Through a friendly Muslim, the missionaries in Tabriz sent food and a piece of matting to Ibrahim, and redeemed for him his cloak, which he had pawned for bread. He was allowed to have his New Testament with him, and most constantly and faithfully did he preach the true life to his fellow bondsmen. He had been thrust into prison for preaching Christ, and yet was allowed to carry on this "criminal" work in the prison itself! One of them, a thief, was so deeply convicted and melted by his appeals and instructions that he made full confession of his sins, and revealed where he secreted certain stolen goods.

The government hesitated to execute Mirza Ibrahim openly lest it should thereby increase interest in Chritsianity, and shake the confidence of people in Islam by letting them see one who had abandoned Islam die boldly for his Christian faith. So he was kept in prison for eleven months at the mercy of an inhuman keeper. After a while he was put down into a moldy cellar, and chained to a gang of murderers, who robbed him of his coat and bedding. But he tried to win even these depraved men to Christ.

One night, after they had been locked up for the night, the prisoners were talking of the two religions of Jesus and Mohammed. His fellow prisoners told Ibrahim that if he did not say that Jesus was false and Ali (the son-in-law of Mohammed) was true, they would choke him to death. By turn each of these base fellows put him to the test, and each time his answer came back, "Jesus is true; choke me if you will." And they did so, one after another, until his eyes bulged out and for minutes he lost consciousness. They desisted without actually taking his life on the spot. But as a consequence of their brutal treatment, his throat so swelled that he could not eat his dry prison fare, and became weaker and weaker. His condition touched even his keeper, and he was moved to the upper prison. But it was too late, and on Sunday, May 14, 1893, he died from his injuries.

When the Crown Prince was informed of the death of Mirza Ibrahim, he asked, "How did he die?" The jailor replied, "He died like a Christian."

He through fiery trials trod,
    And from great affliction came;
Now before the throne of God,
    Sealed with His almighty name,
Clad in rainment pure and white,
    Victor palms within his hands,
Through his dear Redeemer's might
    More than conqueror he stands.

The body of the martyr was buried in a Muslim cemetery in Tabriz, and there was no Christian funeral service. But in later years Christians used to visit his unmarked grave, and thank God for his courage and faithfulness. After some years the cemetery was taken over by the government, and over the spot where Mizra Ibrahim was buried now stands the building of the municipality.

When Dr. Sa'eed visited Urumia in 1891, he met with a group of converts from Islam who had suffered much persecution. One of these was Mirza Ibrahim. Dr. Sa'eed reminded them that from the first Christians had endured tribulation. He told them that the blood of the martyrs has always been the seed of the church, and that Christianity has never been established in any country without some sacrifice of life. He bade them to be prepared, saying, "Who knows for which of us the lot will first fall?" Dr. Sa'eed could not know that his prophetic words would be fulfilled just two years later when Mirza Ibrahim drank the cup of martyrdom.

From such holy seed, from lives laid down in Iran by Mirza Ibrahim and countless other Christians from the first century to the present day, is now growing the church of the Living God.

5

Nozad, New Born in Christ

On February 12, 1905 a former Muslim, who for a number of years had been a believer in Christ, was baptized in the small prayer room in the chapel of the Presbyterian Mission in Teheran by the Reverend J. L. Potter, the witnesses being the Reverend S. M. Jordan and the Reverend L. F. Esselstyn. His name was Rajab Ali. No new baptismal name was given to the convert, but when some years later the Iranian government required all of its subjects to choose for themselves family names, Rajab Ali chose a name which might have been given him at baptism. He became Nozad (New Born), and by that name he is known throughout Iran.

The Reverend William N. Wysham, who knew Nozad intimately in Teheran, wrote thus of him in a Foreword to his translation of the story of Nozad's conversion:

"Nozad became a Christian about thirty years ago, and was one of the very first Moslems in Persia to accept the Gospel. His life has been a varied one, for at different times he has been artisan, steward, attendant in the Parliament during the stormy days of the first constitutional government, city detective, and a trusted employee of the American (Presbyterian) Mission in Teheran. He is largely self-educated, but is surprisingly well-informed, and spends much time in thought and meditation. Keenly observant, he has contributed to a popular Persian magazine a series of articles on conditions in Persia which have been full of wit and satire, and have created much comment.

"During thirty years of Christian experience, this man has been remade by the power of Christ. He is now senior elder in a Persian church (in Teheran) and his power in prayer, his wisdom, independence and common sense are invaluable in the church's growth. In his study of the Bible he has had the help of scarcely any of the wealth of commentaries and spiritual books which we take for granted, but his conception of Christianity is remarkably broad and comprehensive. His life is above reproach, and his quiet efficiency and thoughtfulness are an example to missionaries with whom he works.

"As I write, we are on an evangelistic trip together to one of the smaller cities which is solidly Moslem. He makes a capital traveling companion, and his unending supply of stories and wise observations fill up any empty hours in our days together. He is perhaps at his best when he presents the Gospel of Christ to Moslems who have never before heard it. Fanatics who come to annihilate us with their arguments find that he skillfully disarms their prejudices, and soon they are listening quietly to the old story of the Messiah who was witnessed to by the prophets, taught eternal spiritual truth, and died for our sins. In these discussions he is always entirely fearless in his personal confession of Christianity, though it is still the law of the land that an apostate from Islam shall be killed. . . ."*

Mr. J. D. Payne, for many years the treasurer of the Presbyterian Mission in Iran, writes thus about Rajab Ali Nozad: "Nozad was above all a practical man; he was not an educated man as we would understand that term. He was a man of great wisdom, wide experience, and deep spirituality. His spiritual life enabled him to write the book which was the best seller for many years of all Christian books in the Persian language. This was a manual for use in personal and family devotions. It is still in wide use.

"It was my privilege to be associated with Nozad for twenty years in property upkeep and construction, and general business administration. Hence I feel qualified to say that whatever Nozad said he saw and experienced was seen and experienced by him."

In the year 1927 Nozad published in Persian (he did not know English) the wonderful story of his conversion to Christianity, with the title "How a Human Being May Be Transformed." This record was printed as a booklet outside of Iran, without the name of the author, and was circulated within Iran with great care, lest harm should come to the author, as well as to the work of Christ.

The translation of Nozad's narrative which follows was made by Mr. Payne, who says of it: "The effort has been made to make the translation reflect the thoughts of Nozad in direct translation by words and phrases, rather than by making use of our idiomatic expressions. Hence some of the sentences

* *Moslem World,* January, 1928.

56

seem cumbersome and awkward. This is done to carry over as far as possible the oriental manner of expression."

Thirty years ago, on the last day of Ramazan (the Muslim month of fasting) a large crowd had gathered at sunset to watch for the appearance of the new moon. When the new moon became visible the crowd expressed its joy and rapture, and one of them, in his ecstasy, grabbed one of his friends under the arms from behind and whirled him around. Accidentally, the foot of the friend struck a blow in the abdomen of one of the bystanders and caused such serious internal injuries that he became ill, took to his bed, and died on the third day.

Of his family there remained one son eight years old, two daughters, one six and the other four, and one daughter yet unborn, seven months in the womb of the mother.

He left no savings, so that the widow was compelled to sell her household possessions, and only by the exercise of the strictest economy was she able to support the family until the son grew up. The son, after changing his jobs many times, decided to become a servant, and entered into the companionship of sinners.

All mankind is depraved, but of this period it may be said that the servant class was more than ordinarily vicious. It goes without saying that a depraved person in a depraved atmosphere would engage in nothing but depravity. Since the sins of this young man were beyond description and narration, I will forego setting them down. By way of introduction I will say that I was that young man.

In observing the tenets of the religion of my fathers, I was fanatically zealous — my prayers were said without neglecting the appointed times, the fast I kept, I remembered the martyrs and I went on pilgrimages. My fanaticism went beyond those of my own age, yet sin had dominion over me and I fulfilled all of its desires. Although my heart was unsatisfied and my conscience rebuked me, I was a slave of sin.

After a time I found an acquaintance and friend who was scholarly and learned, and whose equal up to the present I have not encountered. Those who had an acquaintance with this person considered him an extraordinary character. Although he was a recluse, living a life of retirement and always seeking to withdraw himself from mankind, he was a teacher and had pupils from the families of the grandees and aristocrats.

The branches of learning which he taught included medicine, anatomy, history, mathematics, religious jurisprudence, doctrine, metaphysics, physics, chemistry, Persian, Arabic, penmanship, logic, astronomy, and geography. Forty-six years he had studied, 12 years in Kermanshah, 14 years in the Meso-potamian shrines, 10 years in the Academy of Sciences of Teheran, and 10 years in Sabzevar.

About seventy years of life had passed over his head, and in all that time he had not married. Of the possessions of this world he had nothing but a room filled with Persian and Arabic books, of which about 95 percent were written by hand. Other than that he had nothing. Among those of whom he spoke always with respect were Abu Ali Sina (Avicenna) and the theologian Mulla Sadra. A book to which he paid great respect was the New Testament.

By conversing with him I became somewhat acquainted with the universe. I learned four kinds of accounts from him, and some of the elements of geography, astronomy, medicine, anatomy, physics, and especially history, struck my fancy. But every time I brought the subject of religion into the conversation, he feigned ignorance and went off onto other subjects. Finally one day I said, "Why do you seek always to avoid the subject of religion?"

He answered, "If I told you what I know, you would not have the endurance and forbearance to hear it; and if I told you what would please you, it would be contrary to my convictions."

I heard this sort of reply from him many times, and to myself I would say, "What do I want that is contrary to his convictions, or what would he say that is beyond my forbearance to hear?" Finally one day I said to him, "Sir, whatever be the answer to my question, do not withhold it! On my part I promise that on hearing it I will show self-control."

He said, "If you give me such a promise, I will speak; but I do not suppose that you can carry out your promise. However, come what may, tell me what your question is." I said, "Be pleased to tell me what your religion is, and what divine book you know to be the true one."

He answered, "I believe in God who is the Maker of all the worlds; in that I have no difficulties, because this creation cannot exist without a powerful and able Maker whose existence and being are eternal. But I have no belief in any of the persons who have made pretensions to being prophets except Jesus. He withstands me most disconcertingly! For a long time I have tried to resist him, but I cannot prevail."

The hearing of this reply, clashing with my fanaticism, caused my ears to ring, and my feelings to be filled with indignation. Yet I controlled myself and did not show them.

I asked, "Why are you unattracted to the others, and yet are captivated by the Christ?"

He replied, "The others have done works which I can say were possible by the wisdom of men, but the things Christ did are not the work of a man."

I queried, "What were the acts of Christ that were beyond the wisdom of men, that you cannot reject?"

He answered, "They are of great range. One is that the dead cannot be given life by the wisdom of men or legerdamain, or in any other way save by the power of God."

I said, "On what reasons do you base your belief, and how do you know that they are true? Do you have proofs of the validity of your belief?"

He replied, "If there was just one Gospel I might have doubts, but there are four versions of the Gospel; each of the four versions apparently differs from the others. It is evident that the writers of the Gospels were four people, and and it is evident that the versions were not written at one time and in one locality. With these seemingly apparent differences their truth, meaning, and substance are identical. In every one of the four versions the miracles of Jesus are related at great length. And this is solid proof of the authenticity of the book. The deeds of Christ are so universally famous and well known that now in Iran, Arabia, Afghanistan, Turkestan, Egypt, Syria and even some of the countries of Africa, if you ask a physician why he has not cured a certain patient, he will reply, 'Am I Jesus the Messiah that I can give life to the dead?' "

I said, "What do you say with regard to Moses, David, and the others?" He made answer, "I am engaged in study with regard to Jesus, and I have two questions giving me trouble, concerning which I must inquire of the authorities on the Gospel. Whenever these two questions are solved for me, I shall become a Christian. Every Christian must accept the prophets of the Old Testament because Christ has accepted them."

I inquired, "With regard to the Prophet Mohammed and the Koran, what do you say?"

He answered, "Neither in the Koran nor in Mohammed do I see anything that I consider to be from God. Islam is founded on the sword, pillage, blasphemy, obstinacy, selfishness, power mania, and sensuality. There are to be found in it some sayings and precepts which were extracted from the Torat (Old Testament) and the Gospel. What we see and hear today in Islam was made up later and written into the Book under the guise of traditions and sayings. They were not there in the beginning. On the contrary, the purpose was world conquest, burning of books, spreading the Arabic language, destroying the civilization of Persia and Rome (Byzantium), plundering treasuries, raping the young women and killing the young men, banishing the old men and silencing people, and compelling the acknowledgment that there is no god but Allah and Mohammed is his Prophet — but the essential intent was that Mohammed was the Prophet of Allah."

I said, "Sir, the Koran with its greatness, is there not something to be found in it that you acknowledge as the word of God? Perhaps you have not studied it with care."

He smiled and answered, "The greater part of my life has been spent in the study of Islamic learning; in Islam I am a religious leader competent to practice religious jurisprudence. There is nothing in the Koran or Islam that is hidden from me. Whatever of the verses of the Koran you wish I will repeat from memory. I know all the traditions of the Shi'ites and the Sunnites, and the interpretations of the commentators with regard to these verses.

"You know that I never make a pretension without sound basis. I have been to great lengths in my study, and had there been any truth in Islam I would never have given it up. I am not demented, and I am not the enemy of my own salvation. Know this, that any person who has knowledge one-tenth as profound as mine concerning Islam would turn from it, excepting three classes who cling to Islam:

"First, those who gain their livelihood by carrying out its religious rituals; second, those who use religion as the means for furthering their own ambitions, and by this means have found preferment and advancement, or have the hope of finding them through it; third, the common people who have no learning and who accept piously whatever they hear in their own environment without proof or questioning. Without these three classes Islam would not exist.

"The Koran is a book without beginning or end, hopelessly incoherent and bewildering. In it is the story of Solomon and Belghis (Queen of Sheba); in it is the story of the ant and the wind, who are the emissaries of Solomon; in it is the story of the unfortunate Zaid and his faithful wife, who became unlawful for him, but was lawful for Mohammed; in it is the story of Maryam the Copt who was first lawful, then unlawful, then lawful, to add to his (Mohammed's) numerous wives; in it is the cursing of Abu Lahab; in it are commands inculcating murder and plunder; in it are hundreds of stories devoid of truth, unrecorded in history, contrary to logic, contrary to science, contrary to reason, contrary to justice.

60

"These few points I mention as examples. You may accept it or not as you please!"

I cannot describe what happened to me upon hearing these remarks. But I knew I considered it my duty to kill him. All thought of sleep, food and rest left me; night and day I was frantically seeking an answer, and to revenge myself upon him. I could not find repose, because I was positive that everything he had said was blasphemy, and could not be true actually, for the reason that I knew Mohammed and the Koran to be innocent and guiltness of any fault or imperfection. I therefore associated with the ecclesiastics, and engaged myself in a struggle to investigate and ascertain the truth.

After two years I became certain that his statements to me were not defamatory and malicious, but were all true. In the end the religious authorities drew a curtain over them; the commentators by their own theories indicated that truth was in agreement with his statements.

Finally, the lamp of Islam in my heart was extinguished; no matter how much I sought to improve the oil and trim the wick it was to no avail. I despaired of everything and all people, I had no belief in anything. I looked upon the world as a universe without common sense or intelligence. All of the prophets were in my mind impostors, and all of the sacred books I looked upon as so many tattered bits of paper. The creation of mankind I looked upon as a freak of nature, and I said to myself that the life of man was limited to so many heartbeats, which would soon cease; that man was living in a state of transcience; that there was nothing in the world but eternal darkness, and that humanity would disappear in annihilation.

I looked upon the world as a dunghill; I held nothing dear; nothing contented me; I looked upon the world as if it were a laughing stock or a plaything. Every moment of my life passed in the most intense darkness and nightmare. I was expecting death solely and only, and release from the talons of the universe, to slip down into the abyss of annihilation. With the most intense resentment and the utmost sorrow, I brought night to day and day to night. I was not content with life. I said, "Would that I could get away from this masterless world!"

One day it came to my mind that it would be well if I talked a bit with one of the Christian priests, to learn what he had to say — although I was confident there was no person in the world who could convince me. Inasmuch as I was not acquainted with a priest I searched until I found a learned Christian (a Presbyterian missionary); his house was at the edge of the city, and all around it was unoccupied land with no houses upon it. Three times I went to his house, and every time for several hours I conversed and debated with him, but did not get the real meaning of a thing he said.

The fourth time, which was to be the last call I made upon him, I heard these words (from him): "Just as malaria is widespread in the world, and its cure is effected only with quinine, even though it is bitter, in the same way all mankind is sick with sin, and the sole medicine for that is the Gospel. Everyone has the choice of accepting it or rejecting it." That was the end of our conversation.

The noon cannon was discharged as I rose from my place and departed, but in what a state of sadness and disappointment and hopelessness! As I went out of the door of his house, there was nothing but barren land and a few mud walls. There was nothing and nobody, and I saw myself wandering solitary and alone in that desolate place. In a state of complete distraction I raised my hands and said, "O God, if thou dost exist and Jesus is from thee and the Gospel is the remedy for the sickness of the world, guide thou me, for I am in great perplexity! If thou art not, then I have spoken to the wind."

Suddenly I saw above my head two spiritual forms whose countenances and clothing were like the color of the sky, who said in loud tones, "God is, and Jesus is true. Of that rest assured, and come!" Immediately they disappeared.

This vision and this sound threw me into panic. A terrible fear took hold of me, and immediately sweat poured from all over my body. I trembled, and in the heat of noonday I became so cold that my teeth chattered. Immediately I broke into a run till I reached a part of the city that was built up, where people were passing to and fro. When my eyes fell upon human beings, my panic and agitation departed.

But on account of this vision and the voices that I heard, I felt completely certain that I was not the same man I had been at first. All at once dejection, gloom and resentment, desperation and hopelessness fled from me, and a new happiness full of joy and deep tranquility took their place. In truth, I beheld myself a new man, possessing a new life.

I desired to consult the Gospel (New Testament), and when I referred to it the Gospel was not the same Gospel that I had read before, although it was the same volume. I took extraordinary pleasure in reading it; perusal of its verses brought an increase of joy upon joy, and delight upon delight. It seemed to me that all the verses had been written to accord with my desires, my thoughts and my convictions.

Continually I told myself that this is the same Gospel that I had formerly read, then why on that day was it one book, and today another book? In short, for four days and nights I read the Gospel with the greatest diligence. The only part that I found beyond my comprehension was the Revelation of John.

After I had gone over the Gospel painstakingly, I referred to the Old Testament. That vast ocean of inexplicable questions that I had been unable to fathom now became clear to me. I was so happy and joyful that whenever I came to a private place I either danced or leapt, or I quoted or composed poetry.

From that day the Bible became, and still is, my treasury, my riches, my library, my recreation, my joy, the remedy for my hopeless spiritual pains, and the solution of all my difficulties. My hope, my pride, my life, the confidence of my heart, my salvation, my faith, my absolute certainty. My King, my Lord is Jesus Christ, who was crucified, buried, and who rose on the third day, and sits in authority on the right hand of God, who was and is and shall be from the beginning to the end possessed of glory, power, and might.

And this grace, love, compassion and gifts of mercy which are beyond all imagination or intellectual conception or explanation, or the comprehension of all mankind, has come from God who is the Creator of all things and is above all things, to insignificant, unworthy, perverse and undeserving mankind. Let glory, honor and reverence be given to his blessed Name!

This new life washed away all my tears, and took away all my sorrows. Only one cause of grief remains in my heart: why are my fellow countrymen without the knowledge of this grace and joy? My prayer is that God will reveal his light to their hearts so that, putting aside their ignorance and fanaticism, they will come to the blessing, love, and salvation that is given freely and gratuitously to every person who seeks it, in order that all may be the possessors of eternal life.

Afterwards, I desired to become acquainted with my fellow-believers. I searched until I found the house of worship of the evangelical Christians, where each Sunday the Gospel was preached. My occupation did not permit me to be present every Sunday, because I was the steward of a person who had placed upon me the entire responsibility of his establishment. All his business, all his villages, his landed properties, the buying and selling, and the oversight of his household were my responsibility. In fact, I was in his stead. With all this responsibility I made every effort (to attend church), and most

63

Sundays I was present. My master and his sons, his wives and all my fellow-employees, knew me as a Christian, and many times I read the Holy Bible for my master. He viewed it with approbation, although he was not a Christian. He showed no antagonism.

It is necessary to add a few words concerning my dear friend who first made me aware of the truth of Christianity and of the nature of Islam. At a time when I had gone on business to Iraq, he wrote me that he was sick, and said, "If you do not see me again, know that the two questions have been clarified for me; hereafter I am a Christian." When I returned to Teheran seven months later, he had died.

The experiences that have happened to me are many. There are some that I have not told and never shall tell to a human being. There are others which, if I told them with all their backgrounds, would be very lengthy but I shall relate briefly several experiences from a third class.

In those days the ruler of Iran was Mozaffar-ed-Din Shah, and after the Shah the first person in the realm was Mirza Ali Akbar Khan Atabeg the Great. One of the servants of the Atabeg had on a pretext seized some of the possessions of my sister; but I, being an employee of the Atabeg, could not cope with him because the courts and the government sided with him.

One day my sister said, "That man is powerful and I am weak. Is there a way out of this difficulty, or must I despair of relief?" For reply I could only hang my head in shame.

It then came to my mind that it would be a good idea to go to the chapel (of the Mission) and there pray. On Sunday I went to the chapel, and after the sermon I prayed in my heart, "O Christ, thou knowest that other than myself my sister has no one to help her, and I am not able to cope with this powerful adversary. I commit this affair to thee — do as thou knowest best!"

After I had offered this prayer, I came out and went to the house of my employer. On that same Sunday that servant placed all of my sister's possessions on the backs of porters and delivered them to her, leaving without even asking for a receipt. Afterwards I heard that he had said to his wife that if those articles should remain in his house that night it would burn down. The result of this prayer so impressed me that in my heart I was ashamed before Christ, because he so promptly gave me relief from the dire straits I was in.

Not long afterwards, when I was living in the house with this same sister, her fifteen-month-old child had a very large swelling develop in his throat. Gradually this swelling grew

64

until it was as large as the child's head, and the larger it became, the harder it got. Whatever treatment the doctor prescribed, such as poultices and so on, gave no relief. The conditions reached the place where the child, on account of the severity of the pain, could not drink milk, and nothing could do down his throat. He was not able to make any movement of the body. One day they told me that on that night all would be over for the child, because it had not eaten or moved for four days, and no sign could be detected of softening or improvement in the swelling. *a healing*

One hour after midnight I finished my work and came to my house, and asked about the condition of the child. They said he was the same as before. Softly I entered the room, went to the child's bedside, I placed my finger on several parts of the swelling and perceived that it was harder than a green quince. Slowly the child half opened his eyes, glanced at me, and closed them again. I was greatly upset and immeasurable pity overcame me. I passed from my natural state of feeling to an entirely different mood. To sum up, I do not know what happened to me. As Paul said, "Whether in the body or out of the body I do not know" (II Cor. 12:2). I can say that these words came out of my mouth involuntarily, "O pain, in the name of Jesus go out of the life of this child by this hour tomorrow night!" Then I breathed on the face of the child.

After uttering these words a great weakness came over me. I betook myself to one side of the room and sat down, leaning against a roll of bedding. I sensed a sound of movement; I opened my eyes and saw that the child had risen from his place, and creeping and rising was coming toward me. Immediately I took him in my arms and called his mother to give him milk. Surprise and astonishment enveloped me when on that same night the child drank milk, played and smiled. Whenever we touched or pressed on the swelling, it was as if we were pressing on his clothes — he had absolutely no feeling of pain. That night passed with happiness, and early in the morning I arose and went to my work .

An hour after nightfall when I was released from my duties, as I was going toward my house, I was sure that the illness had departed from the child. When I got to the house I looked at the child, and saw that the little melon, that is to say, the large swelling, was gone. My mother said that the swelling had burst of its own accord, and expelled a great quantity of pus, even though at the time the child was busily playing, and the opening closed up so quickly that now only the spot was visible.

I had a fellow worker who considered me his rival, and in our work he took every opportunity to wrong me, but I endured it with patience. After a year an opportunity came to me to pay him back for all his wrongs; but, although my heart was wounded by his conduct, I did all I could to show him good will. My friends said to me, "It is the day of vengeance, do whatever you wish." I said, "Vengeance is God's; my Book tells me not to do evil for evil, so I have committed him to God. I will do nothing else to him except to show him good will."

After several months that fellow worker went to sleep one night in perfect health; in the morning when he woke up half of his body was paralyzed. When I saw this occurrence I was very sorry that I had committed him to God; my duty was to have forgiven him. I have repented many times of this omission, because a Christian must forgive from his heart.

These incidents remain with me as recollections from those days. Each one in its own place plays the part of a band of steel that has made the fabric of my faith more solid. Had these abnormal and unconventional matters not been shown to me by an unseen hand, possibly my natural curiosity would have been satisfied with accepting the teachings of learned men who insist that the whole world is the creation of nature, an accidental happening, an occurrence of natural development, and would have led me into other areas of thought.

But now to all these myriads of important and philosophical matters, when I hear them, my faith replies, "I have become acquainted with God through God himself, and I know that He is always and everywhere present, and all the time sees and knows and hears, and He receives any person who comes to Him, whoever and whatever he is."

I know this because I, who was of human beings the most perverse, the most base, the most unworthy, the greatest sinner, the most unfortunate, the most without resource, most disgraced, most friendless, most obscure, most doomed to destruction, have been received into fellowship through Jesus Christ.

Above all I state from my own experience that the service of Christ causes a person to be strong, to abstain from evil and to accomplish good deeds. The Christian wishes evil to no one; he sympathizes with his fellow men.

Honesty, sincerity, reliance upon God and gratitude are some of the inescapable duties of a Christian. The Christian is in communion with God and always seeks to do his pleasure. The Christian desires and is ready to help others. The Christian is not content simply with knowing what is good and what is bad, but seeks always to forsake the bad and perform the good. A Christian must make his belief and his actions prove each other, so that his conduct may give glory to God in the sight of others. Therefore I lift up my voice and say:

O fellow men! O fellow creatures! Be aware that the salvation of God is free and eternal. Do not sell it cheaply. Do not barter it for things of the world. Do not be negligent.

Life is like a swift-winged dove darting speedily to its final resting place. Its nest has been prepared either in the talons of the falcon of destruction, or in the assembly of the friends of God in the presence of Christ.

God has placed the choice in this matter within the range of our striving and endeavor.

Ask yourself one question: Where are you going, toward death or toward life?

One thing I will say: the wellspring of life and salvation is Christ; you may accept it, or you may reject it.

My prayer is that God will direct the rays of his enlightenment into your heart. Amen.

Rajab Ali Nozad died in 1944, trusting in Christ.

6

The Mirror of the Monarch

When the representatives of the various local churches in northern Iran, which had been founded by the Mission of the Presbyterian Church in the U.S.A., met in 1934 for the purpose of organizing a Synod, the man chosen as moderator was an elder of the Evangelical Church of Teheran, whose title was Merat-us-Sultan, and whose family name was Ibrahimian. The great majority of the 2500 members of the churches in the Synod were Assyrians, several hundred were Armenians, and a yet smaller number were converts from Judaism and Islam. But the man whom they elected as moderator was a Muslim convert, and his election was a striking tribute to the character and ability of one who represented the smallest minority in the church. How did it happen that Merat-us-Sultan left his former religion, and became a leader in the Christian church in Iran? The story is an amazing one, and those who heard it from the lips of the convert will never forget it.

The Arabic phrase "Merat-us-Sultan," which was the title given by the Iranian government to the man whose story we are telling when he was an officer in the army, means "The Mirror of the Monarch." Later, when titles were abolished by the government, and everyone was required to choose a family name, Merat-us-Sultan became Merat Ibrahimian.

Merat was born about 1876. He was not himself a prince, but in his childhood he was a playmate of princes, for he lived in the "anderoon" (women's quarters) of the Shah's palace in Teheran, where his mother was one of the foster mothers in the royal household. During these plastic years he learned much. He became familiar with the noble families of the land as they came and went through the palace grounds. He learned how to handle folks, and how to get things done without offending the person with whom he dealt.

When Merat became too old to continue in the "anderoon," he was sent to school. Later he entered the army and became an officer. His quick wit, his pleasant manner, his executive ability, and his friendships with those of high rank caused him to rise rapidly in his profession. He was an Iranian gentleman of the highest type. He was still young in years when he was sent to Tabriz in northwest Iran, close to the Russian border, to become chief of police of that city. Tabriz was at that time the residence of the Crown Prince, and the second largest and most influential city in Iran. Life for the chief of police was not without its thrills, for Russia considered northern Iran to be her rightful prey, and many were the intrigues into which Merat delved and many the plots and counterplots with which he juggled.

In the Tabriz experience came a pleasant interlude, when Merat returned to Teheran and married the girl of his mother's choice. He had never seen his fifteen-year-old bride, nor had she seen him prior to the marriage. But a week before the wedding he sent her his picture, and the girl liked the looks of the trim military figure, the proud bearing, and the keen eyes in a pleasant, intelligent face. The marriage turned out to be a real love affair on the part of both. When the first baby was born, girl though she was, her parents loved her, and called her Malak Zaman (Angel of the Age). Later three more daughters and two sons were born to the happy couple.

While in Teheran, Merat was one day invited to the home of his wife's uncle for lunch. The host was a Muslim ecclesiastic of high standing in the city. The weather was warm, and after the bounteous feast all the guests lay down for their afternoon nap. But the young officer was not sleepy, so he betook himself to his host's library to see if he could find a book with which to while away the time.

As he idly pulled out one volume and then another, he came at last on a book which had fallen behind the others and was hidden from view. He drew this out, blew the dust from its covers, and looked at the title. It was *Mizan-ul-Haqq (The Balance of Truth).** Merat opened the book and began to read, and he kept on reading. Hours went by, twilight came, and the house became quiet after the departure of the other guests, and still he read. At length the host, in search of his missing guest, opened the door and came in. Merat looked up, and said to his host, "Have you read this book?"

His host smiled, and replied, "That book is all right for me to read for I am a man learned in the doctrines of Islam, but it is not good for a youth like you!"

So saying, he took the volume from Merat's hands, and put

* See Introduction.

it again in its place behind the other books on the shelf. The officer did not see the book again, but its contents stayed with him, and in the years to come he thought often about the striking difference which *The Balance of Truth* had demonstrated between the teachings of Christ and the teachings of Islam.

After a time Merat returned to Tabriz as commander of both the Iranian police and army. It was the time when the paw of the Russian Bear was preparing to strike, and suddenly it came down upon Tabriz. The Iranian troops, ill-trained and badly equipped, tried for a time to resist, and then fled. What happened to their commander can best be told in Merat's own words, in a booklet which he wrote in 1948, a few years before his death, and which was published in Teheran in Persian, with his picture on the front page and the title "How I Was Saved." What follows is a somewhat free translation of the story of Merat-us-Sultan.

In the year 1330 A.H. (1912 A.D.) the Tzarist Imperial Army came to Tabriz from Julfa, in the Russian Caucasus, on the pretense of protecting their Russian subjects, but actually to assist Mohammed Ali, the deposed Shah of Iran, an undertaking which was quite illegal. The insolent Russian army, after entering Tabriz and arresting a number of the religious leaders and influential citizens of the city, hanged them on the gallows in the middle of the drill ground of Tabriz on the Tenth Day of Moharram, leaving this shameful act as a memorial to the despotic Russian government.

After finishing this brutal business, they undertook to arrest the governor and the chief of the Azarbaijan police and gendarmerie in order to execute them also. At this time the governor of Tabriz was Prince Amanullah Mirza, and the chief of police was Merat-us-Sultan. When the Prince governor was informed of this plan, in view of the weakness of the Iranian government, and the distance from Teheran, he gave up all hope of receiving help from the government. And since he had to preserve his honor, there was no choice left to him but to seek asylum in the British Consulate in Tabriz. Finally, he committed suicide.

But after the above mentioned events, I (Merat-us-Sultan) tendered my resignation as chief of police to the Teheran government by telegraph, and fled in disguise by way of the Turkish border to the land of Armenia (in Turkey), and remained for a time in Van, where the governor of Armenia resided.

When I left Tabriz I passed through Meshk-Ambar, one of the Armenian villages, which is situated some twenty miles northwest of Tabriz, and because of the heavy snowfall and the severe cold, I took refuge for a time in the house of the Armenian priest who resided there. After forty days the weather improved, it stopped snowing, and the roads became passable again.

So I prepared to continue my journey to Turkish territory. As I was leaving the house of the priest, my host made a prayer to help the traveller on his way, and then said to me, "My dear guest, during all your stay in my house I have daily prayed in the presence of the Lord Jesus Christ for your salvation from the wickedness of the Russians, and have asked that your journey may be a safe one, and that you may reach your home in perfect health and peace. I am sure that Christ will keep you safe till you return to your household. But are you ready to promise Christ in your heart that when you enter your home in peace you will not forget him, but will commit yourself to your Savior?"

I gave my promise to the priest, saying, "Of course." Then I started on my journey, and the priest with great joy said once more, "Go, and be confident that Christ will save you — but do not forget your promise!"

For many months I was a wanderer and a vagrant in Turkey, a fugitive from the oppression of the Russian government. At last I returned by way of Saujbulagh in western Iran to Zenjan, and journeyed toward Kazvin on my way to Teheran. Three farsakhs (12 miles) before reaching Kazvin I stopped for the night in a teahouse, expecting to enter Kazvin next day. But at midnight the Russian Cossacks captured me in my bed, and took me to Kazvin, and for some time kept me in prison, first in the Russian Consulate, and later in their military camp, intending to send me to the Caucasus for execution.

The military imprisonment in a dark cell lasted a long time. I did not know the reason for the delay, and was day and night expecting the end. One day the lock of the prison door opened, and a Russian army colonel entered and said to me, "Sir, please come!" I went out of the prison with the colonel, and we entered the avenue. Opposite the door of the prison, on the other side of the avenue, a photographer was standing with a camera waiting for us, and as soon as we came up he took two pictures of me, one standing and one sitting. Then he went about his business. After that the Russian colonel conducted me back to the prison, but before he departed he said to me, "Since you are to be our guest for only a day and a night, you may make any request of me that you wish, and I will do it for you."

So I said to him, "Why were two pictures taken of me?"

The colonel replied, "One is to be sent to the Caucasus, and one will remain in the Russian Consulate in Kazvin."

"I am grateful to you," I said, "I have nothing else to ask."

Then the colonel said, "I consider it necessary to introduce myself to you. I am an Iranian prince. It was my fate to go far from my native land, and enter the military service of a foreign government. Now that you know I am not a foreigner, ask me without any hesitation for anything I can do for you, and I will not fail to do it."

I replied, "Since this is the case, I also can make known to you my heart's desire. From the taking of the two pictures of me I understood that the order for my excution has come from Russia. Can you tell me definitely on what day you will get rid of me?"

"Tomorrow, three hours before noon," he replied. The conversation ended, the colonel went out of the prison, and the door was again locked.

In the terrible night which followed, something happened which Merat did not include in his written account, but which he described in later years to his intimate friends. He said that alone in his cell, facing the disgrace of hanging on the gallows on the morrow, it occurred to him that an easier way out of this trap would be to swallow a lump of opium, the favorite method of committing suicide in Iran, where at that time opium was widely used. So he gave the servant who brought tea to the prisoners some money to procure and bring to him enough of this poison to kill him. The servant did his part well, and a lump of opium came into the prisoner's hands, stuck to the under side of the saucer on which the tea glass rested. When the servant had gone, Merat put the opium on the table before him, and looked at it. Should he swallow it?

He thought of the ease with which he could take it and depart this life. How much better than the disgrace of a public hanging at the hands of the hated Russians! But, then, suicide would also bring disgrace to himself and his family. What would those friends of his in high positions in the government of his country think of him if he killed himself like a coward? Would it not be better if they thought of him as having died a martyr's death, of having died as a brave soldier in the service of his country? For hours that night in his lonely cell he wrestled with this problem. No, he simply could not bring himself to swallow the little brown lump with its sickening odor which was lying on the table before him. More and more he felt certain

72

that it would not be right for him to take his own life. If he must die, he would die at the hands of the Russians!

But was death inevitable? For many days and nights, as he had sat in his cell, he had besought help from all the prophets and holy men of his Muslim religion with whose names he was acquainted, but no assurance of salvation had come to him. Now in this last awful hour, when terror had taken possession of his soul, there flashed on his mind like a light in the darkness the words of the Armenian priest, "Don't forget Christ!" At once he knelt, and cried out to Christ, "O Jesus Christ, I have committed many sins in my life. I am a great sinner! But in this matter for which I am about to be executed I am innocent. These Russians are Christians, they are thy people. Don't allow them to commit this crime! I do not know thee now. But if thou wilt save, I promise to seek earnestly to know thee, and when I find thee I will devote my life to thy service!" After he said this, fear left him, and peace filled his heart. With his head in his hands on the table, he slept till morning.

The night ended, and the fateful day dawned. At nine o'clock Merat heard the sound of the Russian bugle, and he knew that his hour had come. But before anyone came to take him out of prison, he once more prayed to Christ. "O Jesus Christ," he cried, "if thou art alive, and if thou art the Savior of sinful men, save me a sinner from this calamity, that I may believe in thee!" *cf Psalmist* —

Now the story continues in the words of Merat's written account.

Immediately after the prayer the prison door opened, and the same colonel who had come the day before entered and said to me, "Please, let us go!" So in the depths of hopelessness and despair, I went forth with him from the prison, and entered the avenue. There I noticed that, in addition to the twenty-five Russian soldiers who accompanied the colonel, a large number of soldiers and Cossacks were on both sides of the street, had taken charge of me, and were moving forward. In front of all the shops on both sides of the avenue, and also on the rooftops, a vast crowd of Iranian men and women had assembled, and were mourning because an Iranian officer in the service of his country was to be executed in his native land by foreigners, and they with their tears escorted me on my way. From seeing this sad spectacle I became so greatly agitated and confused that I completely forgot myself, and saw nothing but the gallows-tree set up before my eyes — unless a miracle should occur.

Of course no one but God could understand my condition at such a time. A prisoner, sentenced to death, like a moving corpse among the surrounding people, moving without any will of my own, I went toward the place of execution. Not knowing what I was doing, I said in my heart, "O Christ, dost thou see how thy people want to hang me contrary to justice? If thou art the Savior, save me!" I was still engaged in prayer as I walked along when suddenly I saw an Iranian officer with twelve Iranian soldiers facing the Russian colonel and the prisoner. The officer placed a letter in the hand of the Russian colonel. The colonel took the letter and read it, then looked at me and smiled, and, taking my hand, put it in the hand of the Iranian officer. Then he and all the Russian soldiers returned to their place.

The officer who had taken my hand said to me, "Aqa* [Sir or Mr.] Merat-us-Sultan, please come, let us go!" and started off, and as we moved along all were silent. After we had walked for about half an hour, we entered the Kazvin police headquarters, and I was taken to the office of the chief of police. Then, pointing to the chair of the chief which was behind his desk, they said to me, "Please be seated, while we inform the governor of Kazvin of your arrival."

When the officer had gone out of the chief's office, I came to myself and said to the attendant, "Who was this officer who led me here?"

"The chief of police of Kazvin," replied the attendant.

This thought then passed through my mind: Since this place is Iranian territory, and the Russians have no legal right to execute an Iranian with their own hands, they have no choice but to deliver me to the governor of Kazvin, that I may be executed by the Iranian government. So the chief of police has gone to inform the governor of my arrival to tell him that he has taken over the prisoner, and to ask him what now must be done. Surely he will return after an hour and they will execute me. Yet I can be glad that I am to die at the hands of Iranians! Since this is the case, it would be well for me to take advantage of this opportunity and write my will, that after my death they may give it to my family.

I at once took from the desk before me paper and pen, and began to write a will. At this moment the chief of police came back from the governor's office and entered the room, and was surprised to see me engaged in writing a letter. He at once came near and inquired, "Sir, what are you writing?"

"Pardon me," I replied, "I am writing my will for my family,

* Aqa is now used in Iran for Sir or Mr.

74

and after my death, kindly send it to them by whatever means you have."

On hearing this the chief of police became greatly disturbed, took the paper from my hand, and tore it up, saying, "God forbid that you are thinking of killing yourself!"

"I have no such intention," I replied, "but you are charged with my execution!"

In amazement the chief answered, "Aqa Merat-us-Sultan, I now realize that you are completely mistaken, and are entirely uninformed as to the course that events have taken. I beg you to drink some tea while I explain the truth of the matter to you."

Then he ordered tea to be brought and, sitting down facing me, he spoke as follows: "From the day that the Russians arrested and imprisoned you, the governor of Kazvin has been kept informed, has reported by telegraph to the government in Teheran all that has happened, and has received instructions to take steps through the Russian Consul in Kazvin to secure your release. The discussions of the Iranian government with the Russian Legation in Teheran, the talks of the governor with the Russian Consulate in Kazvin, and the discussions of the Consulate and Legation with the Russian Tzarist court, were carried on till yesterday but with no result.

"However, last night two telegrams from Teheran were received by the governor, one from the Ministry of Foreign Affairs, and one from the Ministry of the Interior. The contents of both telegrams were about the same, namely, that a strong order had been issued by the Russian Legation in Teheran to the Russian Consulate in Kazvin that Merat-us-Sultan should be delivered immediately to the governor of Kazvin, and at once sent to Teheran. These telegrams arrived several hours after nightfall, when the consul had gone to bed, and at that time of night it was impossible to interview him. So there was nothing to do but wait till morning. Today I was ordered by the governor to see the consul and deliver to him the telegrams about this matter. At 9 A.M. I was able to see him, and I got a letter from him directing that the Russian officers should without delay deliver you to me, that I might bring you here. And this has been done.

"Now I have seen the governor, and he has given orders that we send you to Teheran. You may go to Teheran any hour you wish, but for your safety, lest on the way the Russians should again trouble you, an officer and several gendarmes will accompany you. This is briefly the story of what has happened."

When the chief of police ended his explanation, I inquired as to the direction for worship, and they showed me the direction of Mecca. Immediately I knelt on the ground and put my forehead in the dust, and my tongue uttered these words, which came from my heart: "Praise be to the Presence of Unity and Perfect Power, thou my creator, who for the sake of Jesus Christ hast forgiven me and saved me from death! I acknowledge in thy holy Presence that I have this salvation from Jesus Christ, and I confess and promise, O my God, that as long as I have life, I will be Christ's." Then I lifted my head from the ground and at that moment experienced in myself a degree of happiness beyond the limits of human understanding. I took the hand of the chief of police in my two hands, and said, "I am personally extremely grateful to you! Now permit me to find some means of travel to Teheran."

"Please make any arrangements you wish for going to Teheran," replied the chief, "there will be no objection."

So without loss of time I made the necessary arrangements and, with an officer and several gendarmes, started from Kazvin, and reaching Teheran after two days, I went into the enclosure in which the Court and the Cabinet were located. There I met the Prime Minister and the Minister of the Interior [who had an important part in securing Merat's release]. When I met the Minister of the Interior, he kissed my cheek and said, "Have no doubt about it, the Most High God saved you from death, and in my opinion this is a miracle! Now you must be our guest for a time in the Ministry of the Interior, till we secure from St. Petersburg your freedom from this unexpected entanglement."

My stay in the Ministry of the Interior lasted for a whole year. The Cabinet changed. The new Prime Minister, with the help of the new Minister of the Interior, made earnest efforts on my behalf, till at last in September, 1913, the following telegram came from the Tzarist Russian government: "Merat-us-Sultan is free, on condition that he does not go out of Teheran, and the Iranian government is to stand surety for him." After the receipt of this telegram the matter was ended, and I remained in Teheran a free man!

It was a joy to be once more in his home with his wife and family! There is a well-known saying of the Iranian poet Saadi to the effect that "it is the man who has been overtaken by adversity who can appreciate the value of prosperity." Who could appreciate the blessings of home life more than Merat, who in Kazvin had written his last farewell to his family?

One Sunday morning Merat's wife Bala Khanum said to him, "I hope you don't mind but during your absence I have been going for diversion with a friend to the meetings in the church on Ghavam-us-Saltaneh Avenue."

"No," replied her husband, "but I am sure the preacher says nothing of importance. I could easily silence him!" So Bala Khanum continued to attend the Persian services at the Presbyterian Mission.

Some time after this, Merat one day met in the street an old friend of his by the name of Rajab Ali Nozad. After they had exchanged greetings in the courteous fashion of Iran, Nozad said to him, "Aqa Merat-us-Sultan, at the time you were in the dark prison of the Russians in Kazvin, I too was in that city. I went there to make known to people the Word of God. When I learned that your imprisonment was a very perilous one, I appealed to Jesus Christ as my intercessor before Almighty God, and never ceased to pray for your release until I heard you had reached Teheran in safety. Now I want you to remember that you are indebted to Christ for your salvation from prison and from death."

"My dear friend," replied Merat, "I well know that it was Jesus Christ who saved me! Now tell me what I should do."

"Believe on Christ," said Nozad, "that you may have peace of mind in this world and in the next, and through faith in Christ receive forgiveness of your sins."

On the following day, which was Friday, Nozad conducted Merat to the Presbyterian Mission to meet the Reverend H. C. Schuler and a group of Iranian Christian men who met there each week for Bible study and prayer. Most of these were converts from Judaism and Islam. When Merat was introduced by his friend to the group, he said, "I have been saved from certain death by Jesus Christ. Now I have come here to confess my faith. Please tell me what I must do."

Merat then told his amazing story to the little company of Christians, and they were profoundly impressed. It seemed to them almost as though they had met Lazarus just out of the tomb! When Merat finished speaking, he fell on his knees in the middle of the room, and with tears asked God's forgiveness for not having sooner kept his promise to the Armenian priest and professed his faith in Christ his Savior. Then the Christians gathered about him and, placing their hands on his head, prayed for God's blessing on this new brother in the faith.

Having confessed his faith before his Christian friends, Merat now realized that he must also tell his wife and his relatives that he had become a Christian. But how could he bring himself to do this? The Muslim law requires a woman to leave her husband if he forsakes Islam and becomes an infidel. Surely his wife would leave him as soon as she heard of his change of

77

religion, and his happy home would be his no longer. Yet, whatever happened, he knew he *must* confess his faith in Christ.

One day, while he was still casting about in his mind for a way in which to break the news gently to his wife, she came to him, saying, "There is something between us which separates us, and I must confess it to you. As I told you, during your absence I sometimes went to the church services. My heart was very sad because you were away and in the church I heard words which comforted me. So I kept on going to the church, and I saw that the truth was there. Now I am a Christian! I cannot hide it from you. So do with me what you will!"

For a moment Merat was speechless with joy and shame — joy, because his beloved wife was one with him in faith in Christ, and shame, because she had shown more courage than he in confessing her faith.

A year after he had professed his faith, Merat one day said to his friend Nozad, "Tell me, according to the rules of the church, what else must I do to be a Christian?"

Nozad replied, "You must request baptism from the pastor of the church." So Merat went in person to the meeting of the elders of the church, and asked to be baptized. One who was present at this meeting recalls how Merat, in answer to the question as to why he had become a Christian, told the thrilling story of his deliverance from death by Jesus Christ. Some months later, on November 7, 1920, he was baptized by Dr. Samuel M. Jordan, in the Persian service of the Evangelical Church of Teheran. Five months later his wife was baptized, and in the following years his six children received baptism. He was very eager that his whole family belong to Christ.

Soon after his baptism, Merat sold his house and bought another nearer the church. During this period of his life, Merat did not have any permanent position and was living off his capital. One day he came to one of his trusted brothers in Christ, the Reverend Jollynoos Hakim, missionary to the Jews, bringing with him two heavy tin boxes. "In these boxes," he said, "are 200,000 krans in silver coins. [Silver money was used in Iran at that time. This sum was then equivalent to about $25,000.] I have been offered a high post in the Ministry of War, but since I am a Christian, I do not want to accept it. The money in these boxes is from the sale of my property, and I will use it for our expenses till God leads me to find a position. So please keep this for me!" Mr. Hakim accordingly acted as Merat's bank till all the money had been used up.

When a Muslim becomes a Christian, he must indeed take up his cross to follow his Lord. Merat's experience was no exception, and these early years of his Christian life were far from easy. It was during these times of testing that God gave him several profound spiritual experiences which drew him closer to Christ, and greatly strengthened his faith. He described some of these experiences, which he called "Revelations," in his booklet "How I Was Saved." Here we will give a free translation of three of them.

After the laying on of hands by Mr. Schuler, as I was lying in my bed, I saw myself standing in a vast plain, facing an immense mountain at which I was gazing. On the top of the mountain was a huge palace, and above the roof of the palace a cross was standing. The gate of the garden and of the building was closed from within. Outside the palace, before the closed gate, a man was standing gazing intently at the palace. Just then I noticed someone standing beside me, and at once I said to him, "Sir, to whom does this palace belong, and who is the man standing before the closed gate?"

That unknown person replied to me, "The owner of this palace which you see is Jesus Christ, and that man who is standing outside the gate is Merat-us-Sultan, who wants the gate to be opened to him, that he may enter Christ's palace."

On hearing these words I suddenly awoke from sleep, and for a long time sat in my place meditating, amazed, and dumbfounded. Then I arose to pray, and said, "O Almighty God, thou knowest that I have believed on the Lord Christ from the bottom of my heart, and I recognize as Savior no one but Jesus Christ. What then was the meaning of this discouraging dream, in which the gate of entrance to Christ's palace was shut in my face?"

The rest of the night till morning I spent in prayer. Then when day dawned I dressed and went to the house of Mr. Schuler, and told him the story of last night's dream. On hearing my words, Mr. Schuler at once rose from his place and, bringing a book, put it in my hand, saying, "Read this, that you may be able to interpret your dream." Immediately I opened the book and saw that the title was *Pilgrim's Progress*. I took the book home, and began to read it. On one of the pages of the book I saw a picture of the building on top of the mountain which I had seen in my dream on the previous night, and also I saw the picture of a man standing before a closed gate, looking just like the man in the dream, without a particle of difference. At once I laid aside the book, and putting my forehead on the ground, I prostrated myself and praised God.

On another occasion after my baptism, several of the brothers in the church and I arranged to meet one night each week in the prayer room of the chapel of the Mission and spend an hour in the study of the New Testament and in prayer. On one of these evenings, when with one heart and one spirit we had gathered in the place of worship, we read the Word of God and then began to pray together. As I was engaged in prayer, I noticed that the walls of the prayer room had been taken away, and I saw a vast plain, the whole expanse of which was so filled with a great light that it dazzled the eye. This great light was not from the moon and not from the sun, but, as was perfectly evident, was from the heaven which eye cannot see. In this state of ecstacy I entirely forgot the meeting and the friends who were all engaged in prayer, giving my whole attention to the light, and being enraptured by it.

When I came to my self, and the brothers had all raised their heads from prayer, they shook hands with me saying, "We must go." One of those present, Rabi [Mr.] Yeprem Urshan, an Assyrian Christian, took my hand in both of his and inquired, "Brother, what is going to happen to you? Your face is so radiant!"

I replied, "Didn't you see this light that I saw when we were in prayer?"

"Brother," said Rabi Yeprem, "this is a revelation that has come to you in prayer. Blessed are you."

A third revelation occurred one day when I left my home to go, as my custom was, to the prayer meeting. As soon as I entered the avenue it seemed to me that the soles of my feet were not on the ground when I walked, but I was moving forward in the air. At the same time a great light filled the whole avenue. So strong was the light that I saw that everything within me was bright, and the light had truly illumined my whole being and was radiating brightness before me. Though I was observing everything and was looking at myself and at that spectacle, I never felt any surprise, and it seemed as though I had always been in this sort of world. In this same state of radiant ecstacy I reached the appointed place. All the brothers were present, and the prayer meeting that day ended with extraordinary happiness and joy.

Supposing that all the brothers present in the meeting were one with me in this spiritual state, as I went away from the place of prayer I passed the door of the house of Dr. Sa'eed Kurdistani. Naturally I wanted to see the doctor for he also was one of the enlightened Christians. When I entered the house and saw Dr. Sa'eed, I said to him, "Brother, are you as thrilled by this radiant experience as I am?"

The doctor, on hearing this, replied, "Brother, this experience has been revealed to you not by flesh and blood, but it is the radiance of the wonderful light of God which has illumined you in these days. Rejoice, for you will see more than this, and better than this!" For a whole night and day this spiritual state and radiant ecstacy were mine, and so thrilled was I by the presence of that light in me that my joy cannot be described. God alone knew the state I was in.

It is clear from what Merat has written that not only the mystical experiences which were so real to him, but also the love and fellowship which he found in the group of "Brothers," were sources of very great comfort and strength to the new believer. A friend recalls that once when Merat was speaking to the members of the little Persian church on Luke 18:28-30, he stated that Christ's words had come literally true in his case, for he had had to give up most of his relations and possessions. At the climax of his impassioned address, he threw out his hands toward the congregation and said, "*You* are my parents and brothers — manifold more, I have eternal life as well!" One who attended these meetings wrote, "When Merat got up to pray, it seemed as if he had his hands on God's altar and that he was speaking personally to God. Such sincere fervor from a man of Merat's education and capability, in a Muslim land, made us Westerners wonder why we had not laid hold on the faith as he had."

Though he was in need of regular work, Merat for several years refused to take a position with the Presbyterian Mission in Teheran, since he did not want to do religious work for money. He wanted his service to Christ to be a freewill offering, and was loath to give non-Christians an opportunity to accuse him of having become a Christian for material reasons. So he continued to live off the silver in the tin boxes in the home of his friend.

At length, however, Merat was persuaded to accept the offer made him by Mr. J. D. Payne, the treasurer of the Mission, to become the business manager of the Mission Hospital in Teheran at a modest salary. In this position his work was giving oversight to servants and supplies, and making all financial arrangements with patients. His business ability, his executive power, his wide acquaintanceship, his tact and discretion, his pleasing personality and his flair for making friends were invaluable to the hospital.

In addition to this managerial work for which he was paid, Merat was constantly on the lookout for opportunities to lead men to Christ. From the Bible which was always on his desk, he often read to those who were waiting in his office to see the doctor. Many patients from among his old friends, and people of high position among the nobility of Iran, frequented his office, and he made full use of these opportunities to speak about the joy and assurance of eternal life which he had in Christ.

One of the missionary doctors recalls that, when one day he came from the operating room to Merat's office in great distress to tell him that an operation on a boy's eye for cataract had been a sad failure, Merat tried to comfort him by saying, "Do not grieve so much! Though you were unable to give physical sight to the son in the operating room, I was at the same time bringing spiritual sight to the father in my office, as I told him about Christ the Light of the World."

In the performance of his duties in the hospital, Merat needed to make frequent use of the telephone, and before the day of dial phones he had many conversations with the operators, who were all men. His unfailing courtesy and friendliness so impressed one of them that he resolved to meet the man whose voice he had so often heard over the wire. The result was that the operator became the friend not only of Merat but also of Merat's Master.

In the year 1924 Dr. and Mrs. Philip McDowell and several members of the staff of the Teheran Mission Hospital went by wagon to the town of Kashan to spend several weeks there in medical and evangelistic work. Mrs. McDowell wrote in a letter to friends in America: "I have not told you about the work of the Merat-us-Sultan, who was with us as an evangelist. He is a remarkable man and he did a remarkable work there." And Dr. McDowell in his report on this trip writes: "The evangelist Merat-us-Sultan and Mirza Abdullah Khan (Dr. Vassei) had absolute liberty to preach the Gospel without let or hindrance. There was a genuine desire to learn the truth. These two converts were invited to the house of a religious leader who had the greatest reputation for sanctity and religious fervor in the city, and in the presence of a large audience, they declared the fundamental truths of Christianity, and challenged the mulla to uphold his position. This he was unable to do, so he was given any length of time he might desire to prepare his defense. It was never presented, and the incident became the common talk of the town."

In due time Merat was elected an elder in the Evangelical Church of Teheran, and for many years he was one of the pillars of the church. The Reverend Jollynoos Hakim writes of this service as follows: "As an elder he served very faithfully. His judgment on vital affairs and problems of the church was very sound. He was always ready to attend to duties the

Session assigned to him, even when they were of a kind that others would not accept. Once when one of the converts had sinned and fallen into serious difficulty, Merat was appointed to deal with the matter. The man was required to confess his sin in the church service, which he did. And Merat was so deeply grieved that he burst into tears."

From time to time Merat was asked to preach both in the church services for Christians and in the evangelistic services. He was a most eloquent speaker. Once in a large evangelistic service, when the mission chapel was filled with Muslims, Merat told the story of his deliverance from death by Christ with such dramatic power that the audience was spellbound by his bold testimony. After listening to one of Merat's sermons, Dr. Schuler, himself an eloquent preacher in Persian, remarked to another missionary, "Why can't we preach like that?"

As the number of Jewish and Muslim converts in Teheran increased, the Session of the church decided that, in addition to the public evangelistic service in the mission chapel on Sunday morning, there was a need for a devotional service for Christians only. Accordingly, a number of the Persian-speaking members of the church got permission to erect a building on the mission property, contributed the necessary funds, and built a small but attractice place of worship for themselves. "What joy we had," wrote one of them, "when the building was finished! For several years we used the building for church services, prayer meetings, and meetings of the Session. It was a great blessing to the Christian community. Merat's part in this enterprise was great." During this time the Armenian members of the church held their services in their own language in a separate building.

When the growth of the city of Teheran made it necessary for the church to acquire new property for a cemetery, Mr. Hakim proposed to the Session that a tract of land be bought for this purpose east of the city at Solaymanieh, where Jews, Baha'is and Muslims already had their cemeteries. Merat was deeply interested in this undertaking and more than anyone else worked to develop the property. He chose a particular plot for himself. He prepared his grave with rejoicing, and danced around it, for he believed there is no death for one who is in Christ. He had no fear of death.

"A friend in need," we say, "is a friend indeed," and many times did Merat prove himself to be such a friend. Mr. Hakim tells how Merat once came to his help when he was in great need. Mr. Hakim had arranged an evangelistic meeting in the Jewish quarter of Teheran, and had invited Dr. Schuler to be the peacher. The room was filled to overflowing with non-

Christians, and the interest was great. But as soon as the meeting ended the police sent for Mr. Hakim, and kept him for four days. When they questioned him he told them that he was a Christian minister whose business it was to preach the Gospel, and he emphatically denied the charge that his meeting had a political purpose.

When Merat heard what had happened to his friend, he at once called on the chief officials, and explained to them what Mr. Hakim had been doing, assuring them of his innocence of any political intrigue. He also urged that Mr. Hakim's past record be examined, and when this was done, it was found to be clean. Then Merat begged that Mr. Hakim be released at once, and offered to be detained himself in the place of his friend, should this be necessary. It was not necessary, and on the fourth day Mr. Hakim was permitted to go to his home.

One evening a missionary who had been invited to dinner in Merat's hospitable home was talking with his host before the meal. As he raised his eyes and looked about the room, he saw hanging on the wall a picture of a man in uniform with a stern, cold expression on his face. "Whose picture is that?" inquired the guest.

"Oh, that is my picture before Christ saved me," replied Merat. And pointing to a picture on the opposite wall, he continued, "and there is my picture after I became a Christian!" The guest, looking at the smiling face of one in whose heart was the love of Christ, understood better than before the reality of the change that had been wrought in Merat's life. He had now truly become the Mirror of the Monarch.

In his latter years Merat's health was not good, and when his friends visited him as he sat under his warm "kursi," he was always eager to talk tbout the things of God, and to pray with his guests. Most of his old friends, his brothers in Christ, had died, and Merat felt very lonely. It was at this time that he had another "Revelation," the last one recorded in his booklet. Concerning it he wrote as follows:

One day when I was sick, and was sitting alone in my bedroom, engaged in prayer for release from high blood pressure, I saw that all at once the walls of the room were removed, and a garden the like of which I had never seen in my whole life, neither in Iran nor abroad, took form before my eyes. I saw myself in the middle of a lawn, with flowers of many colors that filled the garden. But however much I considered the character of the flowers and the waterfalls and the beauty of the garden, I did not understand anything about it, for I had never seen anything like it. Then, while I was engaged in gazing at the garden in great amazement, I saw the whole group of brothers, those who on the nights of prayer used to be together and pray together, one by one passing under the trees. As soon as I saw them I looked at them most intently, and noticed that, as they passed at a distance, they saw me and smiled at me and went on their way.

As a result of seeing them, I suddenly became greatly disturbed, and, stretching out my hands toward them, I kept shouting in a loud voice, "My dear brothers, take me with you wherever you are going!" My shouting made them pay more attention to me, and as they passed they smiled at me. But I, amazed that they did not take me with them, kept on shouting louder and louder every moment. These, of course, were the brothers who one after another had gone from this world to be with Christ. Finally, I shouted so loud that my wife and children rushed in terror into my room, and surrounding me sought to find out how I was. When I came to myself, I realized that the garden and all that I had seen was only a vision.

Though several years have passed since this event, I have not forgotten that beautiful garden and the people who passed before my eyes. One of those brothers whom I saw was Nozad, the brother who prayed for me when I was in the Russian prison. Another was Rabi Yeprem, the preacher of the Evangelical Church. And the others were the brothers who used to gather for prayer on the appointed nights of the week. I have no doubt that the spectacle which I saw was the Paradise which has been promised, and always in my prayers I beseech the Most High God that all sinful men may repent and believe on Christ, the only Savior.

A friend of Merat's writes, "I was in the church service in Teheran when Merat told of the vision he had of his dear brothers who had gone to be with Christ. I can see him now as he stood in the pulpit of the mission chapel, describing with dramatic power the passing under the trees of Nozad and the others, and his deep distress that he was unable to go along with them." He could not go then, but not many months passed before he joined them in the beautiful garden.

When he realized that death was approaching, Merat stayed in his room at home and spent his time in reading the Bible and in prayer. He wanted to be alone with his Lord. Death came to him in August, 1948. Most of his closest Christian friends were away from Teheran. Before it was possible to arrange a Christian burial in the grave he had prepared for himself, and in spite of the protest of the pastor of the church, Muslim relatives carried off his body and buried it in a graveyard near the shrine of a Muslim saint. So his desire to rest in the Christian cemetery was not honored by those who had always resented his becoming a Christian.

It has been said that in the Resurrection at the last day many Christians will rise from Muslim graveyards, and certainly one of them will be Merat-us-Sultan. His contributions to the evangelization of Muslims, the building up of the Church of Christ, and the winning of religious liberty in Iran were outstanding.

7

Jalil Qazzaq, Beloved Teacher

Shortly after the death of Jalil Qazzaq in Isfahan on November 26, 1955, a little book was published in Persian which contained a tribute to the life and service of this great Christian, forty pages filled with poems and hymns written by him, and samples of his beautiful penmanship. The author of the book was the Reverend Hassan B. Dehqani-Tafti, who later became the first Iranian bishop of the Anglican Church in Iran.* The Bishop has kindly consented to the translation and inclusion in this volume of a part of his moving tribute to his beloved teacher and friend. He writes as follows:

I was five years old when my mother passed away. The village of Taft where my father lived did not have adequate facilities for education. I was growing up illiterate, like thousands of others. Friends of my mother persuaded my father to let them take me to Isfahan to study. Isfahan is 260 miles from my birthplace. It is a very bitter experience for a seven-year-old motherless boy to say goodbye to his father for the first time, to travel for a long distance, and to be gone for an indefinite period. Even now I recall the flood of tears which rained down from my eyes, soaking my hot cheeks. In those days the road between Yezd, the city nearest to Taft, and Isfahan had been newly opened, and automobiles occasionally went back and forth between the cities. They sat me, choked with sorrow, on a tin can filled with water beside the Zoroastrian chauffeur who was to take me to Israhan.

In those days everyone who wished to enter Isfahan from the south had to cross the Thirty-Three Arch Bridge. It was night when our automobile reached the bridge, and my eyes for the first time beheld the cluster of lights which they had strung in a line across the bridge. Till then I had not seen electric lights,

* In the inspiring story of his own spiritual pilgrimage from Islam to Christ, entitled *Design of My World* (World Christian Books), Bishop Dehqani-Tafti pays eloquent tribute to his old teacher Jalil Qazzaq.

and I shall never to the end of my life forget that beautiful scene. I do not recall where we spent the night, but I do remember that early next morning they brought me to the Hostel of the Stuart Memorial College on Abbasabad Avenue, which at that time was a narrow, dirty alley, and put me in the care of the head of the school.

Where had they brought this seven year old boy? In whose hands did they place him? Everyone realizes the influence of the school environment, and of the personality of the teacher, especially in the early years of a child's life. I am certain that had the teacher to whom they entrusted me in the school on that early morning been any one other than Jalil Qazzaq, I would not have become what I now am. I am not saying that I have now become an important person, or have accomplished a great work. Real achievement consists in this, that one should understand why God has brought him into this world, and should try to live for that. If you accept this definition of achievement, I consider that I have achieved, and at least I can say that I am indebted for finding my way to achievement to my honored schoolmaster, Jalil Qazzaq.

The primary branch of the College had only five classes, with no more than sixty or seventy pupils. Of these, about fifteen lived in the Hostel where I was. Whenever my old fellow-students meet one another, we recall our dear and distinguished teacher, Jalil Qazzaq, and sing his praises and tell of his goodness.

Who was Jalil Qazzaq? He was born in 1879 in Teheran. His father, Khalil, was one of the Yerivan Cossacks (in Persian, "Qazzaq"), who, when Yerivan in the Caucasus was taken from Iran by Russia, considered this separation a wound in the body of the motherland, left all their possessions behind, and moved to Iran. Here they came to the attention of Naser-ed-Din Shah, and attained high rank in his army. When Zill-es-Sultan was governor of Isfahan, it was decided that a unit of the army should be stationed in that city. The commander of this unit, who was aware of Khalil's integrity and faithfulness, invited him to come from Teheran to Isfahan, and appointed him a general. So General Khalil came to Isfahan with his family, and shortly after took up his duties in the new post. Later he returned to Teheran on business, and there fell victim to cholera. So his family, lacking a head, gradually became scattered, but Jalil remained in Isfahan.

The inheritance which General Khalil left to his son was not a material inheritance of lands, houses, gardens and the like. How can an honest government official leave behind him lands and estates for his children? The father had tried to give his

88

son Jalil the finest education obtainable at the time, and in fact had achieved his goal. In addition to erudition in Persian literature, a knowledge of Arabic literature and learning, and an acquaintance with the French, English, and Turkish languages, Jalil had developed a beautiful penmanship, so that he was unquestionably one of the leading calligraphers of the day in Iran. He was also skilled in Iranian music, and played well both the *tar* (a six-string instrument) and the *sitar* (of four strings).

Jalil Qazzaq was not made to be a soldier. He did not enjoy ordering people around, confusion and shouting, place and rank. He had a quiet and humble spirit which from his youth preferred the treasures of quietness, and turned to poems and the writing of poetry and teaching. Because of a lung disease from which he suffered from his youth, he consulted Dr. Carr in the Christian Hospital of Isfahan (established by the Church Missionary Society), and was treated by him. As he had an inquiring mind, he began to study Christianity and the person of Christ. Jalil's family were Sunnite Muslims, but the wonderful personality of Christ, his limitless love in the face of hatred, and the absence of any sort of bitterness or revenge, attracted and charmed him. So in the year 1922, he received the sacrament of baptism in St. Luke's Church in Isfahan, and from then on to the end of his life he counted himself the faithful disciple and unworthy follower of Jesus Christ.

Later, Jalil married a gifted girl named Shokat Khanum, who had been baptized in the same church a year before him. When the branch school and the hostel of the college were opened, none more suitable than Jalil and his wife were to be found for this work of teaching, training and school administration, and they were called to this position. Sad to say, Shokat Khanum, while still young, in the year 1934 returned her spirit to her Creator, leaving behind her, alone in the world, her sensitive and sorrowing husband and three sons. The death of his mate made so profound an impression on the poetic heart of Jalil that from that time to the end of his life he never fully recovered from the shock. In a brief time the family life of this noble family went to pieces. The school and hostel were discontinued, and Jalil was retired on a pension. He lived all alone on his meager pension until on November 26, 1955, after a long illness, he went to his reward with God.

Jalil's funeral we held in the same church in which he had been baptized, and in which he had so often preached. A great number of his friends were present. His body was interred in the Protestant section of the Christian cemetery at the base of Mount Soffeh. That same day Aqa Sepanta, the sweet-tongued poet of Isfahan, composed this poem about his death:

One whose penmanship and poems are unique, beyond compare
In departing leaves his loved ones wrapped in sorrow and despair.
Tho' the pages of his life scroll be rolled up and fade away
The essence cannot ever die and time cannot decay.
If the passing of the years should make his memory grow dim
The pages of his writings still his eloquence will limn.
Even as Jesus after death entered heaven's golden portals,
So has our Jalil Aqa joined the ranks of the immortals.
May his heart live forever, ever filled with tender love!
Jalil Qazzaq still is living in the radiant realm above.

Jalil Qazzaq can be called the father of Iranian Anglicans, not only because of his age, but because of the remarkable abilities which God gave him, and which he dedicated to the church and to the work of God in this land.

First, Qazzaq was a Christian dervish, a mystic and a poet — he was a dervish in the original meaning of the term. He had thoroughly absorbed into himself the best aspects of the civilization and literature of his ancestors, and then had surrendered himself to Christ. He composed many beautiful and eloquent poems, and not merely did he give them a Christian flavor, but he presented in his poems the essence of Christianity. This is to be seen in the hymns which he composed and left as a permanent memorial to the Church in Iran, of which there are about thirty in the current hymnal. This fact is to be seen not merely in the hymns which he wrote, but in his other beautiful odes and poems as well.

Secondly, Qazzaq was a superb calligrapher. A sample of his beautiful handwriting is shown in this book.* His death deprived the church in Iran of its finest calligrapher, and Iran lost one of her best.

In the third place, Qazzaq was a good writer, translator, and preacher. He turned several English books into Persian, which stand as exemplars of his beautiful, simple clear style. One such is "The Highway of the Cross" which he translated in 1948. Another outstanding example is the book called "A Diary of Private Prayer" which he translated from English with his own unique eloquence and clarity.

Some members of the church, realizing how precious Jalil's handwriting is, endeavored as far as posible to make exact productions of books written by him. This was done for the Scripture Gift Mission tracts "The New Law" (the Sermon

* See page 95.

on the Mount), "The Way of Salvation," "God hath Spoken," and other booklets which have been read and admired by tens of thousands of people in Iran. Also Qazzaq wrote the entire Gospel of John in his flowing hand, and it is hoped that this will one day be reproduced and distributed.

If we wish to compress the personality and character of Jalil Qazzaq in a single phrase, we may say he was a combination of emotions, all heart from head to foot, a heart that was grieving, burning, and melting. A small disturbance in life impressed Qazzaq deeply and affected his whole sensitive personality, making his poetic heart to grieve. On this account, especially in the last days of his life, he had a sad and sorrowful countenance and complained of various afflictions. But if one penetrated the depths of his personality, he discovered a kind of happiness, even a jesting personality, and a liveliness that brought to mind the notable verse which Paul writes concerning himself, and which applies equally to Jalil: "As sorrowful, yet always rejoicing; as poor, yet making many rich; as having nothing, and yet possessing everything" (2 Cor. 6:10).

Qazzaq had a pure, clean heart; he never gave way to bitterness and spite toward any, either in word or deed. He got along well in every circumstance and with everyone, and loved everyone. While he always spoke plainly and frankly, he never spoke harshly or offended others. He was not two-faced, never practiced deceit or hypocrisy. Even though he was witty he never spoke evil of his friends behind their backs. But what really made him a great man was his genuine modesty and humility, which came from the communion of his spirit with God. He spent the best days of his life in the work of the church, and perhaps more than any other person served outstandingly. Despite this he was never heard to say that the church did not appreciate him, because he well knew that the church is composed of individual members and not of a few leaders. He expected favors of none, he never slandered, he did not criticize the church. He was well aware of his own weaknesses and mistakes, but his loving and gentle heart and his pure and refined spirit hid only the faults that to some extent afflict every individual.

Of Jalil Qazzaq's company one never had enough. His alertness of mind even till his last days was remarkable. Even though he complained of pains and illnesses and of life in general, still he loved life, and was interested in news from near and far. He had a special attachment to home and family, and frequently recalled with appreciation his father's love for him.

Jalil Qazzaq was a man who loved beauty and nature. He

appreciated beautiful natural scenes, and avoided darkness and isolation. He loved beautiful poetry, and one can almost say that he adored his own handwriting. From one of his poems it is evident that in his youth he was fond of exercise and sports.

> Young was I. Have you fathomed the meaning of youth?
> Youth, the crowning glory of God's gardens forsooth.
> Proud was I of my prancing steeds of Araby;
> Dashing o'er field and dale, peerless in rare beauty.
> Wide and free we roamed wherever the heart pleased,
> The springtime earth radiant as Hesperides.

Even though in the middle of his life he became physically weak, yet to his life's end he had the true spirit of an athlete and the sportsmanship that accepted defeat gracefully.

Very few had as much to do with foreigners as did Jalil Qazzaq. He was intimately associated with the missionaries in Isfahan. But in contrast to those who, after a few contacts with foreigners, forget themselves and put away their own language and customs, he completely retained his true Iranian spirit: dignity, good nature, hospitality, pleasure in society, readiness in repartee and witty expressions, the retaining of friendships, and more than all, warmth and affection were elements of his character, none of which were lost as a result of his relationship with foreigners. While those qualities and customs of the foreigners which do not suit us Iranians never became a part of his nature, at the same time he was loved and respected by all, whether foreigner or Iranian.

There is no question that Qazzaq was immersed, so to speak, in Christian convictions. He was very familiar with the Bible, and in his poems and hymns he expressed Christian principles in the very finest way. He was a Christian in character and conduct, and was ever in communion and fellowship with God. Those who were with him during the last days of his life heard him speaking constantly of "dear Jesus" and the church. Church attendance was for him a regular and fixed matter, and until near the end, when his body no longer permitted him to worship in God's house, he was regularly present in the church services. To him the church was God's house, and not the place for attending to personal business. He expected no favors that might result in complaints, and if by chance there was cause for complaint he did not blame it on the church. And he impressed this good quality on others as well, especially the young men who from their childhood were with him. In all sincerity one must say that he was a friend of Jesus. He testified to this clearly wherever he was, and tried to live according to the standards of his Master. He was by his conduct one of the finest of evangelists.

Finally, something must be said of Jalil's strong liking for his students. He loved his students sincerely, and without favoritism, giving them the greatest encouragement, and this he did to the end of his life. When his students were grown and had their own occupations, he still carried on correspondence with them and through his letters inspired and encouraged them for service. Aqa Abdul-Masih Shirvanian, one of his former students, writes:

"Nearly twenty-eight years ago I lost my mother, and my father brought me from Shiraz to Isfahan and placed me in the College branch school. At that time I was only seven years old. My grandfather was one of the pillars of the Shah Ne'matullahi sect of Sufis, and from my youth I was an admirer of the Sufi path.* Jalil Qazzaq, who was himself a Sufi-like Christian, attracted me, and through him I became acquainted with Christianity. Since he was neither two-faced nor hypocritical, and showed himself a Christian outside as well as inside the church, he taught me by his actions the lessons of sincerity and consistency. Because he was an Iranian patriot, Christianity took on for me and my fellow-students an Iranian color. Contrary to those who say that Christianity is a foreign religion, I became convinced that it has no national limits. So an Iranian can become a Christian as well as a follower of any other faith. I have carried on a regular correspondence with my honored teacher, Jalil Aqa, and I have preserved his letters. I would like to quote from one of these, which he wrote me from Isfahan, one designed to encourage me to persist in God's work till my last breath:

> Dear distinguished son, Aqa Abdul-Masih,
>
> I am extremely happy in your activities and the manly persistence you display in God's service. Truly, whenever I remember that as a result of the ten or twelve years I spent in school work and in running the Hostel, two young believers surrendered to the Lord and today labor in this way for the progress of the work of the church, I thank God with heart and soul that at last the seed sown for this purpose has come to fruition. You and Aqa . . . . are ready with firm faith to undergo every hardship, and I do not know how to express my delight and inner joy. No day passes, whatever my condition, without my praying especially for you two!

Obviously, receiving such letters from my dear old master

---

* The sufis are the mystics of Islam.

93

made a deep impression on me, and encouraged me to continue my service with a single purpose."

This is the testimony of one of Jalil Aqa's old students, showing the influence of that honored man on his character. On first acquaintance, few of the above qualities became evident. One had to live with him and know him intimately to see the deep qualities of his character, and to praise God for them.

On that day, when I at seven years of age, filled with a world of wonder, crossed for the first time the Thirty-Three Arch Bridge and went to the branch school of the College, I did not know that I would be coming under the influence of such a great, pure, believing and talented person. From God's viewpoint, is life other than this, that a man should live for others, and pass on to others whatever he has gathered? Those who want life for themselves, who are constantly thinking about gathering wealth and possessions, seeking rank and position, and even knowledge and learning for selfish purposes, and who do not share these things with others, truly are dead. But those whose goal is to give to those who have not, and then pass on, are never dead but shall live forever. "After death seek not my dust in the tomb, my tomb is in the breast of wise men." Jalil Qazzaq was such a person.

A sample of Jalil Qazzaq's calligraphy is here reproduced. It is the Persian version of the old tradition of the Church of the East about Jesus' comments regarding a dead dog, as related by the poet Nezami of the twelfth century. The verses have been translated thus by the Reverend R. N. Sharp of the Anglican Church in Shiraz:

Jesus within the market place one day
Beheld a dead dog lying in the way.
    A crowd, like crows collected round the corpse,
Flung words of loathing at the noisome clay.

Said one, "As breath snuffs out a candle light
This charnel breath engulfs my soul in night!"
    Another answering said, "What gain we here
Save only sickened hearts and stricken sight!"

So each in turn took up the damning strain,
And heaped upon the dead reproaches vain:
    Until it came to Jesus' turn to speak.
Whereon He straightaway showed the moral plain:

"He that hath eyes to see, behold this sight:
This creature's teeth, than all thy pearls more white!
    Dwell not on others' faults nor thine own grace,
But humbly search thy heart, and there make right!"

دیده ٔ رعیبْ دگران کن فراز   صورت خود بین و در او عیب ساز

پای مسیحا که جهان می‌نبشت   بر سر بازاری چه یکی می‌گذشت

مرده سگی در گذر افتاده بود   یوسفش از چه بدر افتاده بود

بر سر آن جیفه گروهی قطار   بر صفت کرکس مردار خوار

گفت یکی وحشت این در دماغ   تیرگی آرد چو نفس در چراغ

وان دگری گفت اگر حاصلست   کوری چشم است و کبلای لا ست

هر که از این پرده نوائی فشرد   بر سر آن جیفه جفائی نمود

چون سخن نوبت عیسی رسید   عیب رها کرد و بمعنی رسید

گفت ز نقشی که در ایوان اوست   در سپیدی که زه چو دندان اوست

عیب کسان منگر و احسان خویش   دیده فرو بر بگریبان خویش

نمونه ای از خط مرحوم قزاق

8

Khadijeh, Dreamer and Poetess

If it is difficult for a man to become a Christian in Muslim lands and follow Christ faithfully, it is usually yet more difficult for a woman. This will be seen most clearly in the following story, which was told by Khadijeh Jan-Nesar herself in Persian in the year 1955 to her friend Miss Vera Eardley, a missionary of the Anglican Church in Isfahan. Khadijeh was born in Isfahan about 1880.

My father (may God have mercy on him!) was a very good and spiritual man. In our house was a library, which for those days was quite large, and among my father's books was a volume which I afterwards knew to be a Bible. Sometimes I used to ask him, "Father, what is that book?" He would answer, "That is of no use to you now; you shall read it when you are older."

My father was a bookbinder, and he had a shop near the Madreseh-i-Nurieh (Muslim theological school). All about were other trades connected with the school — copyists, bookbinders, illuminators, etc. My father was a kind man, and was strict in keeping the Muslim law. To the end of his life he had only one wife, my mother. I had two brothers and three sisters, the youngest of whom was quite blind and died without marrying when she was only twenty-two years of age. I myself was married at eleven years of age, but did not go to live with my husband till later. My first child was born quite late, when they began to think that I was barren. He was a son, and I was then sixteen. My husband died not very much later, and before long I was married again.

At some time during those years I went one day, closely veiled, with a friend to the dispensary attached to the British Consulate in Isfahan. When my friend went into the room of the Armenian doctor, I waited outside. There two nice Armenian girls who had come from Julfa, the Armenian suburb of Isfahan, to visit their brother made friends with me. Before

96

we left, one of them gave me a little picture of Saint Mary
with the Holy Infant in her arms. I loved that picture and
made a little velvet bag for it, and for many years wore it
next to my heart. I was then about twenty-six years old.

Later I had a very vivid dream, as I was sleeping in my
father's house with my blind sister beside me. In my dream
I found myself wandering in the bazaar, and I had quite lost
my way. As I wandered I came to the door of a big mosque,
and when I entered I saw that it was full of people all dressed
in white. They were sitting on the floor, and were listening
to the preacher who was in the high pulpit. I managed to get
closer, and then saw a woman with a sweet face sitting on the
second step. I asked, "Who is that?" They told me that it was
Saint Mary, the mother of Jesus. But the preacher I could not
see, for from the knees upward he was hidden in a bright,
shining cloud, and his face did not appear. I asked Saint
Mary, "Where is my way home?" Then she told one of those
nearby to show me. He led me out and through the dark
streets. Suddenly I recognized the street we were in and
said, "Take no further trouble; I now know where I am." He
put a bunch of herbs into my hand, saying, "Saint Mary told
me to give these to you." Then he departed. I found my way
home, and then I awoke. I told all this dream to my sister,
and she told my father. My father was able to interpret dreams
and he told me that its meaning was that I should have a
child who would be a great blessing to me, and a source of
much joy. Later on he said, weeping, "Alas, you will become
a Christian."

One day when I had again been to the clinic at the British
Consulate, I had another dream of Christ in which I clearly
saw his face. A man showed me a big, framed picture, and
said, "This is Jesus." As I looked, the Being in the picture
stood before me as a small child, and then he gradually went
up and up, borne aloft by two hands, the owner of which
I could not see.

Soon afterward I went with a friend to the English (Mission)
hospital, to which I had never been before. The lady Bible
teacher (Miss Braine-Hartnell) was reading to waiting patients
from the Gospel, and when she was called out of the room,
I picked up the book she had laid down to see what was
written in it. One of the patients scolded me, saying, "Don't
touch that!" "Why not?" I replied, "a book is for reading."
At this moment the teacher came back and asked what the
talk had been about, and I told her. "Can you read?" she
asked me in surprise, for at that time very few women could
read. But my father, being well educated himself, had taught

us all to read. The lady teacher then gave me the book and said, "Read it to us." I read where she had opened it: "He that loveth father or mother more than me is not worthy of me . . ."

"Do you know about Jesus?" she asked me.

"Yes," I replied, "he is one of the greatest prophets, and to him God gave a heavenly book, the Injil (Gospel)."

Then she asked, "Whose son was he?"

I replied, "He had no father!"

"Really, is that possible?" she asked. Then I told her what we Muslims believe about Jesus. We talked a little more, and then I asked her to give me a picture of Jesus Christ. I wanted to see if the face I had seen in my dream had really been Jesus. "Come again on Wednesday," said the teacher, and she gave me a note to show at the door of the hospital so that they would allow me to enter.

Accordingly, I managed to get away from my home on the excuse of visiting my father's house, and came secretly to the hospital. The lady teacher had not forgotten, and when the door was opened, an old Christian maid-servant was waiting to receive me and to tell the teacher I had come. The teacher took me to a little, quiet room where we read the Bible together and talked much. She also explained to me about the picture of Jesus. "There were no cameras in those days," she said, "and people have drawn the Savior as they think he might have looked." I was disappointed. But she told me to read the book she gave me till I had a picture of Jesus in my heart. At one point she said, "Who do you think Jesus Christ is? We believe him to be God." She saw my color change at this, and then very gently explained it to me. She gave as an illustration the sun, and its light, and its heat — yet all *one* sun.

When I left, the teacher said to me, "Try to come every Wednesday." This was very difficult for me to do, as I was closely watched. My family, and especially my mother who was a very strict Muslim and more severe than my father, had begun to suspect that I was really interested in Christianity. But with one excuse or another I nearly always managed to get to the hospital on Wednesdays, or some other day, to have a lesson. Sometimes I would go to the house of a friend named Fatemeh on the excuse of learning English, and there would meet Miss Biggs (of the Anglican Church) and learn more from her. The mother of my second husband guessed what I was doing, but she was quiet and timid and did not try to stop me.

My mother, however, was determined to prevent me from

becoming a Christian. One day my mother-in-law invited Fatemeh to tea. I went out to get some cakes the day before she was to come, and then went to my father's house to spend the night. The cakes were on a shelf, and my blind sister touched them and asked me what they were. I told her, and she told my mother. Whereupon my mother came in and broke up the cakes. I had no opportunity to buy others, but managed to arrange them on the plate so that the ones most broken were underneath. When I offered them to the guests I felt very much ashamed, but of course could not explain.

In the middle of my tea party my mother suddenly arrived. She spoke very sternly to Fatemeh, saying, "Neither I nor her husband want her to continue these English lessons, and it is against our wish that she is having them." This was very difficult for me and I felt humiliated. When the guest had gone, my mother stayed on. There was a brazier of burning charcoal on the floor between us. My mother said to me, "Can you stand being burned with fire? You will surely go to hell-fire if you are a Christian. Let me see!" She then took a red-hot ember with the tongs and placed it on my wrist. I said, "God gave the fire, and he will also give the power to bear it." And so I bore it, until it had burnt through my skin, and my mother took it away. She loved me, but could not bear the thought of my becoming a "blasphemer."

After that I was made to go to my father's house every week, and a mulla came to teach me that Islam is the true way. I used to stop my ears. Gradually my family began to treat me as ceremonially unclean, and my sister refused to eat from the same bowl with me. My father used often to weep.

About this time I had another dream. In my dream I saw a great field, and at the end of it a high wall reaching to the sky. The field was filled with a vast crowd of people. Old Khorshidjan, the maid-servant who had opened the hospital door for me, was there, and I said to her, "What is this?"

"This is the Day of Judgment," she replied.

"What must I do?" I asked.

"Nothing," she said.

"Then what is the great wall?" I inquired.

"That is the wall of the church," she replied, "and presently Christ will appear above it."

Then I saw a great six-sided throne in the air, and two birds that flew under it, lifting it on their wings until they had placed it above the wall. A Being was sitting on the throne. Presently a great chain was let down, and the cry went up, "Who longs for salvation?" I took hold of the chain, but as I was on the way up, my ring caught on the wall.

99

However, I reached the top, and there a dervish sprinkled sweet-smelling water on me three times. When I woke up, I could still smell its sweet scent.

On thinking about the dream, I understood that the catching of my ring against the wall showed some hindrance, and that I must have no deep heart-attachments. I told the dream to my sister, for I wanted her to understand. But as she dreaded my becoming an infidel, she told my father. When he heard it he wept and said, "Khadijeh has gone from us! Either they are going to baptize her, or they have already done so." But my mother said, "Let us go on a pilgrimage to Karbala,* and take her with us; perhaps that will change her." My uncle wanted to go to Mecca, for since he had the necessary funds for the journey and sufficient money to support his family for a year, the longer pilgrimage was obligatory for him. It was therefore arranged that he should accompany us to Karbala in Iraq, near Baghdad, then go on to Mecca while we waited for him in the holy places of Iraq, and after that return to us and travel with us back to Isfahan.

I had for some time before this been managing to get out and go to the home of Miss Annie Stuart (daughter of Bishop Stuart) for meetings, and usually my mother-in-law came with me to keep an eye on me. This she wanted to do, although she was too frightened to report to my husband what I was doing. Miss Stuart had said to me, "Try not to go to Karbala." But I was forced to go. I had to leave behind me my little daughter Maimanat, aged five. She stayed with my mother-in-law, who loved me and was always afraid my husband would divorce me. We left Isfahan in the late summer (about 1910), and were a big caravan. I and my mother, my uncle and his wife, and many others, both men and women, all rode in "kajavehs" (roofed-in boxes fastened to either side of a mule, in each of which a traveller would sit). I had an uncle at Karbala, my mother's brother, who had an important post as clerk to one of the great men in the sacred shrine.

One day in the bazaar of Karbala I saw two foreigners, and wanted to run after them. My mother hit me and pinched me, and stopped me from doing so. Long afterwards it seemed to me that they must have been Dr. and Mrs. Schaffter (who served for many years in the Isfahan and Yezd Mission hospitals). For when I told them about this many years later, they told me that they had been in Karbala that year, and when they tried to give copies of the Gospels to people, the

* At Karbala is the shrine of the martyred Imam Hosein, grandson of Mohammed, who is highly revered by Shi'ite Muslims.

books had been snatched away and torn up. My mother said to me that day, "I brought you here to try and change your ideas, but alas! one can take Jesus' ass* even to Mecca, and when it gets back, it is still an ass. How can we cure you!"

We stayed in Karbala all through the winter and spring until the party had returned from Mecca. Then we all set out again, and reached Isfahan in the early summer, having been away nine months. First I spent some time in my father's house. While we were away my mother-in-law had died, and my little Maimanat had been looked after by her unkind and jealous aunt. I wept that there had been no one but her to care for my Maimanat, and that now my kind helper had gone.

Meanwhile, my husband's sister had tried to persuade him to take another wife. One day he found his mother, who was really ill, weeping. "What is the matter?" he asked her.

"Your sister wants to marry you to someone else," she replied, "but I want my dear Khadijeh back again!"

He answered, "I don't want another wife." And there for a time the matter remained.

After the death of my mother-in-law, a messenger came one day from the house of Miss Stuart to ask why I did not come to see her. My sister-in-law replied, "Khadijeh is at her father's house," and sent Maimanat with the messenger to show her the way. She gave me the message, but of course my mother knew about it. After the messenger had gone, my mother took me and Maimanat back to my husband's house. There she tied Maimanat's feet and hands together, and beat her with a piece of wood for a long time, to punish her for helping to give the message. She was then only six years old.

When I got home I found that all my papers and books had been destroyed. But my Bible was safe. I had hidden it in a high, dark corner of the cellar. They told me they had looked for it but had never been able to find it.

Maimanat, my beloved daughter, had true love for Christ. When she was nine years old, it was suggested that she should be given in marriage to a cousin of hers, but he was only fifteen years old. So she was not married until she was ten. Her husband was an illiterate and bigoted man. When she was about twelve years old, she used to come with me to the Mission hospital, and one day they gave her a Gospel. She took it home and hid it under the ground. Her husband found it, tore it up, threw it down the lavatory, and beat her with his belt.

*The mother referred to the well-known Muslim tradition that Jesus always rode on an ass, and to this stupid animal she likened her daughter.

She cried, but said, "I'll get another Gospel!" One day he came home from his workshop moaning because he had hurt his hand with his shoemaker's awl. When Maimanat said "Thank God!" he became furious, and inquired, "Why do you say that?"

"Not only," replied Maimanat, "because you are merely wounded and have not lost your hand, but also because you have been punished for throwing the heavenly book down the lavatory." Maimanat had a lot of spirit, and was always fearless.

Meanwhile my good father and my blind sister had both died. That was about 1918, the year of the famine. My brother Ali Reza had joined the dervish sect called Ne'matullahi, and sometimes my mother went with him to the place of their worship. One day she asked the head of the order what their duty was toward me, who had become a Christian. Was I unclean? "No," he said, "she is not unclean. Show her love and kindness, and bring her back to the true path in that way." After this my mother was kinder to me. But my sister-in-law was always unpleasant. She was a hard, jealous woman. She spent much time with me at my husband's house and watched me.

At length I was baptized. On one Saturday evening Dr. Stuart and the Bible teacher, along with Maimanat and a few other friends, took me into the church, and there Bishop Linton baptized me. I wrote the hymn, "To Thee I Come, Receive Me," for my baptism. The words are as follows:

O true Revealer of the love of God,
O Thou who art the Christ, the Son of God,
Spirit of God art Thou, yea, very God,
    To Thee I come, receive me!

O Friend more dear than life itself to me,
Distressed am I and helpless, hear my plea!
By Thy great mercy, Lord, my Helper be!
    To Thee I come, receive me!

I've heard Thy gracious word, "Come unto me
That peace and rest I may give unto thee!"
So at thy portal seeking security
    To Thee I come, receive me!

Jesus, Thou Art my only resting place;
On Thee I call, O hear me by Thy grace!
Never from Thee will my feet stray apace.
    To Thee I come, receive me!

The First art Thou, and Thou the Last wilt be;
All inner meaning, all that eye can see;
Most beautiful and pure in Thy Divinity,
    To Thee I come, receive me!

My sister-in-law, who for years had tried to persuade my husband to take another wife, at last succeeded. She was a servant without any culture or education, who had worked in my sister-in-law's house. She was installed as his wife, and I was given another little room, and had to wait on her. She being a vulgar, coarse woman did everything she could to make me miserable, and made my position as difficult as she could. My husband was away from home a good deal. He was a tax-collector in one of the Lenjan districts, fifteen miles up the river from Isfahan.

For my Maimanat also life was becoming increasingly difficult. She had become pregnant again, but lost the baby, a boy, when her husband in a bad temper hit her and frightened her. While she was in the hospital, her husband took another wife, a rich woman. So when Maimanat came out of the hospital, she refused to go to her husband and went to her father's house. Later she was baptized.

At length we were both divorced by our husbands. We rented a little house together in a street at the back of the bazaar, and there we were happy together. Now and then Esmat (the daughter of Maimanat) was allowed to visit us, and even to stay for a few days. Later on, as we were badly-off financially, my daughter, who was full of energy, was helped to get a camera, and set up as a photographer. We rented two upstairs rooms near the Shah Mosque, behind the great square, and hung up a sign to say she was a photographer. The sign had a cross on it to show that we were Christians.

Here the story of Khadijeh as told by her comes to an end, and what follows has been added by her friends.

Khadijeh Khanum continued as a faithful and devout Christian until her death in 1957. Esmat grew up and married, and she and her husband went to live in the oil fields in south Iran, and Maimanat lived with them. Then Khadijeh went to live with her son and his two wives. Her gentle, sweet face showed nothing of her difficulties at home, for neither the son nor his wives showed her any consideration or affection, even when she was obliged to spend some weeks in the hospital with asthma and bronchitis. Nor did she lose her gallant spirit and quiet sense of humour. She contributed two more hymns to the inter-church hymnbook, written in poetry of high merit.

One winter when she was seriously ill in the hospital, she realized that she was probably going to die. So she told her Christian friends that she wished to have a Christian funeral, and that after the funeral her family should be notified. Usually the Muslim relatives of a convert insist on taking the body, performing the Muslim rites of purification, and burying the deceased as a Muslim.

When Khadijeh's heart failed and she died, none of her relatives were present. So immediate preparations were made for a Christian service in the nearby church, and a message was sent to her family. Meanwhile orders were given for a grave to be dug in the Christian cemetery outside the city, in case the family should allow a Christian burial. There was a fine service in the church, with a goodly number of Christian friends present, and two of the hymns which Khadijeh had written were sung. Many people were weeping, but there was none of the loud wailing usually heard at a Muslim funeral.

As the procession came out of the church, it was met by Khadijeh's son. He thanked the doctors and nurses for their trouble, and said that now he would be responsible for what was done. He had brought a hearse, and took the body away to receive the ritual cleansing which would wash away her apostacy, in the hope that God might forgive her and have mercy on her soul.

Several nights later the crippled woman evangelist in the hospital dreamt that Khadijeh came to her and said, "Why were there so few people at my funeral? It should have been properly announced so that a great many people could have come. It was a great opportunity to give the Christian message. And there was another thing — why did you sing the first line of the hymn I wrote incorrectly? It doesn't make sense!" The evangelist told people of this dream, but did not know what had been sung incorrectly, or that in the hymnbook used at that time the first line actually had been changed from Khadijeh's original version. The difference was not great, but the change was not satisfying to the poetic sense of the author! The line has now been corrected in the 1961 edition of the hymnal.

Khadijeh Jan-Nesar is still loved by all who knew her. She was the stuff of which martyrs are made, on which the still very young church in Iran is being built.

9

Hasan, Spiritual Pilgrim

Few newborn babes have ever received a colder welcome
into this world than that which was extended to little Hasan.
On the day of his birth his own mother cast him out into a
snowdrift to die! It was not that she did not want a child,
for what mother in Iran would not rejoice to bear a son, and
so win her husband's favor? But at the very time that Hasan
was born, word reached his mother that her husband, a merchant who had gone away on a journey, had been murdered
by robbers. She was a woman of strong passions, by race a
member of the fearless and independent tribe of Kurds in
northeastern Iran, whose brother had been a notorious robber
in that region. So she attempted to expel the bad luck from
her house by killing the baby who had brought it on her.
But God had work for this little boy to do, and he did not
die in the snow. Compassionate neighbors picked him up and
placed him in his mother's arms, saying that perhaps the report
of her husband's death was not true, and if he should return
alive to his home he would naturally be very angry and disappointed to discover that she had cast out his child. The
mother listened to reason and kept her baby. How glad was
she that she had done so, for after a time her husband returned safe and well, and she was able proudly to present
him with a son and heir! The baby was named Hasan, the
name of a grandson of Mohammed.

It was in the city of Meshed, in the great eastern province
of Khorasan in the land of Iran that Hasan was born. The
exact date of his birth is not known, but it was about the year
1869. Meshed, which means "Place of Martyrdom," was so
named because many centuries ago the Imam Reza, the eighth
in descent from Mohammed, was there put to death by his
enemies. His grave soon became a place of pilgrimage for
Muslims of the Shi'ite sect, and now for a thousand years
untold multitudes of men, women and children, coming from

105

all parts of Iran and also from distant lands, have visited the sacred city. With joy they welcomed their first glimpse of the great golden dome which covers the tomb of the Imam, glittering like a ball of fire in the sunlight! And with tears and supplications they entered the sacred precincts and kissed the place where the Imam lies, hoping that God would accept their pilgrimage and forgive their sins! Those who made the pilgrimage won the title "Meshedi." The shrine, located at the center of the old city, has always been the very heart of Meshed, and has become very wealthy from gifts and legacies.

As there were no modern schools in Meshed, Hasan, on reaching school age, was sent by his father to a *maktab,* an old-fashioned school in which the pupils sat on the floor, and spent years of their lives memorizing the Arabic Koran, and learning nothing else, sometimes not even learning how to read and write their own beautiful Persian language. Hasan memorized the verses of the Koran, and then when the teacher began to drill him in the very tedious and difficult method of learning the Arabic alphabet, the little boy could not stand it and ran away from school. But the teacher caught him and gave him a beating. Then Hasan put tobacco in his own eyes, and made them so sore that it was impossible for him to use them for study. And that was the end of his schooling!

After that, his father put him to work. He became an apprentice to a goldsmith, then to a butcher, and later to a merchant. When he was about twelve years of age, he became a shepherd and was with his father's flocks for two years. He wandered with his sheep all over northeastern Iran, and learned to love desert life. He used to suck milk from the teats of the goats, and at night would listen to the howling of the wolves.

Later still Hasan became a seller of jewels, and learned to know precious stones well. He liked this trade very much, for it gave him an apportunity to associate with all kinds of people. And it was from association with people, not in the classroom, that Hasan got his education.

The people of Meshed had great faith in the power of the Imam Reza to perform miracles. They said that the blind who visited the shrine received their sight, the sick were healed, and many other wonderful things happened there. When Hasan was a boy he used to have a part in some of these miracles. He and his friends would go to a caravanserai where camels, weary from their journey, were kneeling on the ground in repose, quietly chewing their cuds. These young Muslims took with them a supply of burrs, and by skillfully placing them under the tails of the camels while the keeper was dozing, they

106

were able to cause a sudden revolution in the attitude of the poor beasts. Leaping up from the ground, they would rush out of the gate of the caravanserai and down the street, and it took only a little guiding to route them direct to the sacred shrine. Into the courtyard the camels would run, and the gate-keepers would welcome them, and all the trumpets would blow, and the announcement would be made that a miracle had occurred — camels had made the pilgrimage to the shrine! Naturally Hasan soon became somewhat skeptical of the Imam's miracles!

When Hasan was 24 years of age his father died. Being without work and without money he left Meshed, and went north to Turkestan, which had become a part of the great Russian Empire. There a merchant found him in dire need, gave him clothing and work, and later sent him to Bokhara to another merchant. This man put him to work in his kitchen and told him to cook dinner. Hasan knew little about cooking, so when he tried to boil meat and onions together, he spoiled the food. The merchant then taught him both how to cook and how to trade. After a while he found fault with something that Hasan had done, so Hasan left him, and returned to Iran as penniless as when he went to Turkestan.

After a time he went back to Turkestan, and found work as a day laborer. A confectioner took him as his apprentice, but when Hasan learned that his master was a Baha'i, he left him, for to Hasan Bahai's were heretics. The Baha'i religion stems from the belief of Muslims of the Shi'ite sect that Mohammed was succeeded, one after another, by twelve of his direct descendants, known as "Imams." They say that eleven of the Imams died as martyrs at the hands of their enemies, the Sunnite sect of Islam, but they believe that the Twelfth Imam is alive. They say that he disappeared but did not die, and will one day return to rule the world. He is called the "Mahdi" (Guided) and the "Lord of the Age." In 1844 a young man in Shiraz made the claim that he was the long-expected Twelfth Imam. He was called "The Bab" (Gate) and many accepted him, and were known as Babis. There were uprisings in which thousands of Babis and Muslims were killed. Finally, the Iranian government had the Bab executed in Tabriz in 1850, hoping thus to end these troubles. Later in 1866 one of the devoted followers of the Bab, who had been exiled from Iran to Turkey, publicly made the claim that he was a "Manifestation" of God, and the successor of the Bab and also of Mohammed and Jesus and the previous Manifestations. He took the title "Baha'u'llah" (Splendor of God). Most of the Babis accepted him and became known as

Baha'is. Since the followers of this new religion were often persecuted by the Muslims of Iran, some of them emigrated to Russian territory, where they would have more freedom. In Eshkabad, Turkestan, they built a temple for their worship.

After leaving the Baha'i confectioner, Hasan worked for a month with pick and shovel on the railway line, then went to Samarkand. Here he was employed by another confectioner, who also was a Baha'i, though Hasan did not know it. One day this man said to him, "They killed the Lord of the Age!" "Where?" asked Hasan. "In Tabriz," replied the Baha'i, referring to the execution of the Bab in 1850. On hearing that the Lord of the Age had been killed, Hasan began to weep. "Don't weep," said the Baha'i, "his successor is alive!" "Where is he?" inquired Hasan. "In Akka (Acre), in the Holy Land," said he, and he explained that Abdul-Baha, the son and successor of Baha'u'llah and the head of the Baha'i Movement, was living in Palestine and could be visited there. Hasan's master used to read books to him about the Baha'i religion and talk to him, and then send him out to split wood and build the fire and sweep up the room and work in the bakery.

At this time Hasan was good material for any missionary to work on. He had seen so much wickedness in Muslims that he had largely lost all faith in the religion of his fathers. Formerly he had been very strict in the observance of the prayers and the fasts and the customs of Islam. He once told how on his first trip to Turkestan he had nearly died of thirst, because he thought the drinking cups used by the Russians were unclean and he refused to drink from them. But now he had become quite lax in the performance of religious duties. He was seeking, however, for the true religion, and used to pray that God would guide him. The Baha'is did all they could to convert him to their faith, but they never quite succeeded.

After a time Hasan became ill, and was unwell for six months. Finally he decided to leave the confectioner, and his master paid him three *tomans* (about $3.00) for two years service, and let him go. He had, of course, received board and room free of charge. He took this money to Aqa Musa a Jew, and Musa gave him some tea, and told him to take it to the tea houses and sell it. He did so, and from this small beginning he worked up a good business.

Seeing how he was prospering, the Baha'is tried harder than ever to capture him. One of them offered to let him have his daughter to wife, and Hasan was willing. Before long the father proposed that nineteen people form a company to make cakes in Iran and export them to Russia for sale (19 was the sacred number of the Baha'is). Hasan agreed to provide money, and gave him $600. A factory was set up, but the nineteen men could not work together, and the company went on the rocks. Hasan did not get back a cent of the money he had invested, nor did he get the girl! So he went back to selling tea.

After a time the Baha'i who had treated Hasan so unfairly set fire to his own house, and then blamed Hasan for the conflagration. As a result, Hasan was kept in prison for a month but was finally proved innocent. When he was set free, he said to the Baha'is, "Now I'm going to Akka and fix you!" So to Akka he went, both for the purpose of complaining to Abdul-Baha of the conduct of the Baha'is, and also to investigate the Baha'i religion and see if it were true.

It was a very long and difficult journey from Russian Turkestan to Palestine, a distance of some 2000 miles. Hasan went through Teheran to Baghdad, travelling by wagon. There his money was exhausted, and the rest of the way he went on foot. He made his expenses as he journeyed along by making birds out of paper and selling them to children. "I used to sell four birds," he said later, "and with the money I would buy bread and eggs. Then I would say to my feet, 'Carry me three *farsakhs* (12 miles) and I'll give you food to eat!' I made my body do its work first, then I fed it." In this way he crossed from Mesopotamia (Iraq) to Palestine (Israel), as Abraham had done before him. And two years after setting out on his journey he reached Akka on the Mediterranean Sea.

When Hasan walked into the bazaar in Akka he met there an Iranian who asked him why he had come to Akka. He replied that he had heard there was a man in Akka who claimed to be God, and if this man differed even by a gram from the rest of mankind, he was ready to obey him. The Iranian was a Baha'i, so after conducting Hasan to the caravanserai where they received guests and helping him to get clean again after his long journey, he took him into the meeting of the Baha'is. Abdul-Baha was not present.

Hasan was of course eager to see Abdul-Baha himself, but the Baha'is made him angry by telling him he could not do so without special permission. When he learned that Abdul-Baha had gone to Haifa, some miles south of Akka, he set out on foot to find him. However, the Baha'is, not wanting to seem inhospitable, sent a carriage after him to take him on his way, and he finally reached the Baha'i guest house on the slope of Mt. Carmel, near the beautiful tomb of the Bab. As he was sitting in the midst of a company of believers, Abdul-Baha entered the room. All the Baha'is arose, but Hasan remained seated. Abdul-Baha at once noticed him and said, "Good for

109

you, you have come! Now rise so I can see you." And he took the traveller into his own room and gave him tea, and asked him about his journey from Samarkand.

Shortly after this Hasan began to have a chill. He had malaria, and every three days had chills and fever, and this was the day for the chill. He lay down on the carpet and the Baha'is covered him up. The fever passed, and as he was having a sweat, Abdul-Baha came to him and raised the blanket which he had pulled over his head and said, "Come and have dinner with me." So Hasan got up and went to the table with Abdul-Baha and an Arab guest. After dinner Abdul-Baha said to his followers, "Give this man some quinine." When they did so, Hasan said to them, "It would be better if Abdul-Baha would say to me, 'Have no more chills!' and thus heal me by his word." "The sick must take medicine, and the sinners must pray," was their reply. Hasan took the quinine for a few days, then tired of doing so, and kept on having chills as before. He reasoned that if Abdul-Baha was as great as he claimed to be, why did he need to prescribe medicine like an ordinary person?

Hasan stayed in Akka and Haifa for seventy days. During this time Abdul-Baha showed him numerous kindnesses, taking him riding in his own carriage, and giving him presents of candy and cakes. But the stay in Akka was not a happy experience for Hasan. He was disturbed by the lack of kindness shown to the poor who came to the door of Abdul-Baha's dwelling seeking alms. He was shocked when Abdul-Baha cursed and struck a careless servant. And he failed to find the water of life for which his soul had so long been thirsting. The disciples of Abdul-Baha used to say to him, "Do you realize how much Abdul-Baha loves you?"

"He is very kind," Hasan would reply, "but he is not the Truth (Haqq) as you say he is — that is someone else!"

At last Hasan decided to go back to Iran. When Abdul-Baha heard of his intention, he sent for him, took him into his inner room, and talked with him in private. "By which road will you go?" asked Abdul-Baha. "By way of Damascus," replied Hasan. Then Abdul-Baha rose and took Hasan in his arms and said, "I would like to have you always with me, but since this is a time for service, I send you on your way." Then he instructed Hasan that, if the Baha'is whom he saw along the way should ask him anything about what he had seen at Akka, he was not to tell them and should say he had only passed through as a traveller. The reason for this direction was that the Turkish government, which was then in control of Palestine, was watching Abdul-Baha very care-

110

fully and he was afraid they would find out his real claims for himself. In Akka he used to say the Muslim prayers as though he were a Sunnite Muslim, and did not let it be known publicly that his father had claimed to be a Manifestation of God, and the founder of a new religion which would take the place of Islam. Finally, Abdul-Baha got Hasan a passport, and presented him with two Turkish liras and a Tablet (special letter), and sent him away.

When Hasan reached Beirut, he gave the Tablet to a Baha'i, who considered it a great treasure. Stopping in Aleppo for a while, he sold needles and thread to make some money. When he reached Baghdad he avoided the Baha'is, and thenceforth had nothing more to do with them. Later he reached Teheran, and became an asistant to a merchant for two years, and then he returned to Meshed.

This journey completely disillusioned Hasan, and left him with no faith whatever. After having lost faith in Islam, he had hoped that he might find the Truth in Baha'ism or in some other religion. Now as he returned to his native land, he was in the deepest despair. Abdul-Baha had utterly failed to meet his need, for he saw that he was a sinner like himself. All his long journey had been in vain, and his heart was still uncomforted. "There is no God, and there is no Truth!" he said bitterly. He ceased to pray and to hope, and for several years he was a man without faith in anything. The one thing that Hasan brought back from his pilgrimage to Akka was a title. Muslims who visit Mecca are thereafter called "Haji" (one who has made the Hajj, or pilgrimage). People supposed that this long journey had taken Hasan to Mecca, so after his return he was called "Haji Hasan." He accepted the title!

Returning to Meshed, Haji Hasan joined his brother Gholam Hosein in business. But his brother dealt dishonestly with him and robbed him of a large sum of money, and all his efforts to get justice done him ended in failure. So he opened a little shop and began selling straw. He did not enjoy this business but made enough money to buy a donkey, and became a broker for merchants.

After a time Hasan decided to leave Meshed again, and taking with him a supply of turquoises from Nishapur, he traveled to Tiflis in the Caucasus, and there made his living by selling jewels. He made three journeys from Iran to Tiflis with jewels. All this time he was living in spiritual darkness. Perhaps the nearest he had ever come to Christianity was when he went to a Russian church in Baku and lighted a candle. He had been engaged in smuggling merchandise into Turkestan, and fearing lest he should be caught, he made a vow that if God took care of him and blessed his business, he would express his gratitude by lighting a candle, as the Russians did. His prayer was answered, and he kept his vow. But the candle did not dispel the darkness from his heart. Then one day, all unexpectedly, the light burst upon Haji Hasan. God found him!

On one of his journeys Hasan came to Krasnovodsk, a port city of Russia on the eastern shore of the Caspian Sea. He went on business to a caravanserai, and there he saw a man with a supply of books to sell. It was Benjamin Badal of Iran, the famous colporteur of the British and Foreign Bible Society. Badal spoke to Hasan, and invited him to sit down and listen while he read from the Bible to him. Hasan did so, and the portion which Badal chose was the 24th chapter of Matthew. Hasan became deeply interested in what he heard. Here was a prophecy that false prophets and false Christs were going to come, and would lead many astray. He knew who the "false prophet" was — it was Mohammed! He also knew the "false Christ"— it was Abdul-Baha, who claimed to be Christ come again. Since this prophecy had been fulfilled, it was evident that the one who spoke this prophecy was true. Who was he? Jesus Christ. Then concluded Hasan, Christ is the Truth, the Savior of mankind! How quickly his active mind and hungry heart leaped to this conclusion! From that moment Hasan considered himself a Christian. Badal could not realize how great would be the results of that brief meeting with Hasan! He gave the eager inquirer a copy of the Gospel of Matthew, and went his way.

Hasan gladly took the book, but since he was illiterate, others had to read it to him. Later he came to Resht in northern Iran, and there met Christians and professed his faith in Christ. Hasan's spiritual pilgrimage ended at last. We meet him again in the next chapter as "Stone The Conqueror."

10

Stone the Conqueror

Though Hasan never doubted that Christ was his Savior after his confession in Resht, as told in the previous chapter, he experienced years of vicissitudes in both his business and his spiritual life before he was baptized. He spent four years in Teheran, then went back to Resht. While in Teheran he asked the Rev. H. C. Schuler to baptize him but Dr. Schuler felt that he was not ready. Finally Hasan returned to his old home in the shrine city of Meshed. During his long absence, an American Presbyterian Mission had been established there, and the missionaries soon became his friends. He was fearless in denouncing Islam in fanatical Meshed, so the missionaries advised him to go to Nishapur, the city of the famous poet Omar Khayyam, three days wagon journey west of Meshed. Through the years Hasan had picked up an elementary knowledge of dentistry, so he was given a set of old dental instruments in order to practice dentistry and preach the Gospel. He rented a little building in the Nishapur bazaar and there set up business. To all who visited him he spoke about the inadequacy of Islam and the sufficiency of Jesus Christ and encouraged them to read the Scriptures, piled on a table in his little reading room.

Before long letters came to the Mission in Meshed from a man in Nishapur with whom Hasan had become acquainted, saying that he wanted to become a Christian, and asking that a missionary be sent to instruct and baptize him. It was decided that the Reverend William McE. Miller should go, so in September, 1920, he made the journey by donkey to Nishapur in company with an Iranian Christian. There they met the new inquirer and Hasan. They were both eager to be baptized, and so on October 3 a little service was held in the home of the inquirer, and he and his son and Hasan received baptism. These were probably the first Muslim converts ever to be baptized in Nishapur. It was a great occasion for all the little company, and Hasan was overjoyed that he had at last received baptism after years of waiting.

When Mr. Miller baptized Hasan he did not know that he, like many of his fellow-countrymen at that time, had been addicted to opium for some twenty years. For nine months after his baptism he continued to smoke the drug, and since he kept this habit secret from his missionary friends, no one told him he ought to quit it. Finally he went one day to the opium den and stretched out on the floor with a number of other addicts for his daily smoke. The attendant brought him the pipe, and as he put it to his lips, the thought came to him, "These lips of mine have eaten the Bread and drunk the Cup in the Lord's Supper. How can I pollute them by smoking this filthy thing?" He at once laid down the pipe, and arose to go. "Your opium is not yet finished," said the attendant. "I don't want it," replied Hasan. And from that time he quit opium and never used it again.

After Hasan became a Christian he decided to change his name, since Hasan was a Muslim name. So he asked his friends to cease calling him Haji Hasan, and instead to call him Mansur (Conqueror). This was a name well suited to his unconquerable spirit. Later when Reza Shah Pahlevi ordered all Iranians to choose and register their family names, which many did not have, Mansur consulted his friend Dr. Rolla Hoffman, the director of the Mission hospital in Meshed, about the choice of a family name. He was reminded that Simon had been called Peter, a Stone (which in Persian is *sang*). This name appealed to Mansur, so he registered himself as Mansur Sang (Stone the Conqueror).

When he received this family name, Mansur insisted that it be officially recorded that he was a Christian, and the Muslim official reluctantly wrote down his religion as "Masihi" (Christian). He had this written also on his identification card which he carried with him. To Mansur it seemed impossible that a Christian could conceal his faith, for his chief glory was that he belonged to Christ. On a ring which he always wore he had a seal with a cross at the top, and the words "Christ's Slave Mansur" engraved under it.

No one who heard Mansur's brilliant conversation, in which he quoted Arabic sentences and Persian verses by the hour, would have guessed that he could not read or write, but such was the case. After he became a Christian, he felt the need of being able to read the Bible for himself, and so while still in Nishapur he hired a man to teach him to read. In a week he had mastered three chapters of the Gospel of Matthew, so that he was able to read them fluently, either with or without

114

the book! Then his lessons were interrupted, and he never resumed them. But these three chapters, two, three and four, proved very useful to him. Ever after, when he wished to instruct some individual or read the Scripture in a public meeting, he would open the book to one of these chapters and recite the passage from memory. He was able to quote many chapters of the Bible without the aid of the book, but he found it useful to "read" from the book at times, for this impressed people more. Later he began to have doubts about the honesty of this procedure, and largely stopped opening the book when he recited the Scriptures.

Not long after his baptism, Mansur had to leave Nishapur. His attacks on Islam aroused the ire of the Muslim ecclesiastics, so he followed the injunction of his Lord (which became his practice during the years that followed), "When they persecute you in one town, flee to the next." Thus began his tireless missionary journeys to all parts of Iran. He never again had a house of his own. Without any family ties to hold him in one place, he wandered far and wide. From village to village he would go, out toward the border of Afghanistan, or up north toward Turkestan, or into the salt desert of central Iran, always on the road. Walking with a heavy pack of books and medicines on his back, riding on a donkey, picking up a ride in a truck, any way and every way he got about the country. In the ice and snow of winter, and in the heat of summer, he kept on the move, coming back to Meshed from time to time to see his friends and give his reports, and to get new supplies of Scripture portions. These booklets he called his "seed," and he thought of himself as a "sower" scattering his precious store on all kinds of soil. He visited and distributed Scriptures in many places where no Christian had ever gone before. He openly attacked Mohammed and the Koran whereever he went, so it is not surprising that he was driven from place to place, and that his life was often in danger. His friends urged him to be more conciliatory, but it was difficult for him to restrain his fiery tongue.

In addition to his "seed," Mansur carried in his pack a supply of simple drugs, an enema, and forceps for pulling teeth. For the relief of stomach ache he gave soda, for fever he gave quinine, and the other items of equipment were used as needed. At a time when there was no medical care of any sort provided for the poor villagers, Mansur's coming was often a godsend. Once a crowd gathered about the room where he was, and began to call for the *hakim* (physician). Mansur said to them, "I am not a *hakim!*" "Oh, yes," they replied, "for us you are!" Out of gratitude people often gave him food or money or gifts (he never asked for remuneration), and he was thus able to live as a self-supporting evangelist.

Mansur's method of healing was different from that of other doctors. While he gave drugs and simple remedies, he depended for results not on these material means but on prayer. He said that he did not undertake to treat a patient unless he felt it was God's will that he do so. But whenever he was led by God to accept a patient, he gave his whole attention to the sick person, and to prayer for him. While he was thus engaged he could neither eat nor sleep. When he gave his medicines he always gave a Gospel portion also to the patient. He claimed that every person whom he had treated in this way had recovered.

Though Mansur delighted in speaking to eager crowds of listeners and broadcasting his Gospel "seed," his most effective work was with the individuals whom his magnetic personality attracted to him. Many times he appeared with some needy soul in tow, and would give himself without stint to helping this man. If the person was an addict to drink or opium, Mansur would gird himself for the fight, and devote himself wholly to the task of saving his friend.

On his journeys Mansur was often guilty of criminal neglect in his care of himself. Sometimes he would go several days without any food, and when he did eat he would consume enough to kill an ordinary man. He said that once when he was making a tour of the villages he received in payment for his medical services two dozen eggs and some butter. Not wanting to add these provisions to his already heavy pack of books and medicines, he proceeded to eat them all up, and then in the strength of this nourishment he walked all day long. When he reached his destination and asked how far he had gone, he was told that he had covered more than fifty miles!

The old saying is that clothes make the man, but in the case of Mansur Sang just the opposite was true. Mansur was forever coming out in some new style of dress! It seemed as though his restless spirit must ever be trying to express itself in new and interesting ways. At the time of his baptism he wore a long coat such as was worn by business men of that day, and his face was clean shaven, except for a long mustache which he dyed black. Two years later he returned from India with a full white beard, and saffron-colored turban and robes, looking like an Indian *sahdu*. Later still, when he was travelling in the deserts to the distant villages, he adopted a shepherd's rough wool cloak, and allowed his uncut hair to blow in the breezes. John the Baptist must have looked just like that when he appeared in the desert! Then he cut his hair, trimmed his beard, put on a short coat and an old foreign cap, and wrapped puttees about his legs, thus adopting Western dress long before the Iranian government required the men to wear short coats. The one item which was constant was the shoes. Mansur had a huge pair of very heavy army boots, much too large for him, and these he wore for years. He feared that if he put on lighter shoes, the strength would go from his feet and he would be unable to march long distances, as he had so often done. He always carried a cane.

Mansur followed literally the injunction given to the apostles for their journeys in Galilee to take with them only one shirt. "Once when I was with him in Bujnurd," wrote a Meshed missionary, "I felt quite unhappy because my fellow-worker was dressed in rags. He often resented any attempt to give him financial help, for he did not want it said that he was getting pay for preaching the Gospel. So I hesitated to buy a new shirt for him, much as he needed it. However, matters finally reached such a point that I felt it was imperative that Mansur change his shirt, so one day I handed him some money and firmly bade him take it and buy himself a new garment. He did so, and before long appeared in a new clean shirt. I expressed my job in seeing him so neatly clothed, and he smiled with pleasure. Then, opening his collar, he said 'Yes, I put it on over the other one!' And sure enough there was shirt number one, still holding its own place nearest his heart! I suppose he could still say that he had only one shirt.

The return of Mansur Sang to Meshed after weeks of wandering in the deserts and among the villages of Khorasan was always an event. Mrs. William McE. Miller thus describes his coming:

"Mansur was lean, weather-beaten, very fit in physical endurance of hardship. He required less baggage and sustenance than anyone I ever knew. He resembled a sand-flea by being constantly on the go. He travelled hundreds of miles through scorching desert wastes, and blistering summer sun. Over mountain passes he would go, and find snow-bound travellers huddled together in some tea-house till the storm cleared. I never could decide whether he took to this life because he relished it, or because of supreme devotion and a high sense of honor. Probably it was because of a combination of these reasons. Certainly he revelled in his accounts of his experiences when he returned to Meshed for a time of refreshment.

"Mansur was greatly loved by the children, and they hailed his sudden and unannounced appearances as robins do the coming of spring. 'Mother, Mother,' they would chorus from the garden, 'Mansur's come back!' Mother would rush to the window to see. Yes, there he was, the jolly old fellow, laughing and singing at the top of his voice, waving his cap or hat or sun-helmet, whichever type of headgear he had last acquired on his latest journey (I think he never returned twice with the same article). There he was, pirouetting around on the path, his head thrown back, and the wind ruffling his thinning iron-grey, wispy hair. We all rushed out to greet him, and bring him in to have tea, and to hear some of his latest stories and adventures.

"If the children's father was at home when Mansur arrived, he and Mansur would, after vociferous kissing and hand-shaking, march arm in arm into the house, going straight to the downstairs bathroom, where Mansur could clean up a bit and get rid of the dust, plus lice and fleas, picked up along the road. Then after a while he would emerge from his bath, with pinkish color in his cheeks and fresh garments on his weary body. His eyes, bright fiery brown and very penetrating in their glance, sparkling with pleasure and the excitement of his welcome and the prospect of tea, wandered over us all with a keen and loving glint. He would laugh aloud suddenly and joyously, just because he was back among friends again, with a store of good stories to tell. He was a narrator of adventure par excellence! My only regret was that his language was so picturesque and colorful that my foreign ear missed many points I desperately wanted to get. His speech was flowing, descriptive, full of similies and illustrations.

"Mansur always liked to repeat his adventures, from start to finish of his long trip. He had a marvelous memory, such as is accorded those who never learned to read. Every episode is stamped with photographic accuracy upon the mind, and may be reproduced in conversation with great ease. So it was with him! He could talk for two or three hours at a time, and next day he would pick up his story again, and continue it to the end of his trip, which may have lasted weeks or months."

The Reverend W. N. Wysham of Teheran recalls Mansur's welcome by his children. He writes, "Our children will never forget the wooly puppy he carried in his arms for nearly a thousand miles, in order to fulfill a promise made them months before. The bus was jammed with Muslim pilgrims on the way to a shrine, and they must have made it extremely miserable for this old man who insisted on keeping an unclean dog in their midst. Doubtless he used the incident to preach to them by the hour of the Christ who had done away with ceremonial uncleanness in his saving work of grace."

Mansur was acquainted with the Christians in Meshed and Teheran, but he had not visited the other churches in north and central Iran. He was, therefore, eager to make a grand tour in which he would meet his brethren in all the cities, sow his "seed" and give his testimony in all parts of the land. There was no problem about financing this journey, for Mansur planned to travel on foot, or to pick up rides in wagons or trucks, and he would trust the Lord to provide food and shelter, as he had always done. So confident was he that the Lord was his Shepherd and he would not suffer want, that he never asked his friends for financial aid. He gloried in paying his own way, and often refused gifts of money from those who wanted to assist him. And he frequently embarrassed his missionary friends by giving to them the presents which his patients had given to him.

Accordingly, supplied with letters of introduction from the missionaries in Meshed to those in other cities, Mansur set forth in the spring of 1929 on a memorable journey of several thousand miles. Everywhere he went, his old friends were delighted to see him again, and he made a host of new ones. He also brought inspiration to a great many people.

He was on the road steadily from May to September, making stops in Teheran, Zenjan, Tabriz, Urumia (Rezaieh), Hamadan and Kermanshah, all of the stations of the Presbyterian Mission except Resht. From each city letters came to Meshed telling of his adventures enroute — his constant sowing of literature as "seed" and his difficulties with the police — and describing his welcome by missionaries and Iranian Christians. In the fall he went south and was warmly welcomed by Church of England misionaries in Isfahan and Shiraz. He remained in Shiraz from December to April, 1930, and the Reverend J. R. Richards of the C.M.S. station there wrote that "Mansur came along like a refreshing breeze." On his part, Mansur found in Mr. Richards a man after his own heart.

Thirty years after Mansur's death, when Mr. Richards had become Bishop of St. David's in Wales, he recorded some of his experiences with Mansur during this period and on later visits. He writes: "One afternoon we visited the tomb of Hafez, the great poet, taking with us Scriptures to sell. The tomb is in a garden which was a favorite resort of a dervish group, and some of its members were there when we arrived. Mansur approached them and asked if anyone was interested in buying a copy of the Scriptures. One of them replied: 'We already have the Holy Book, and better copies of it than those you are selling.'"

"I'm glad you have copies," replied Mansur, "and I'm interested to hear that you have better copies than these I am selling. Are they leather-bound, by any chance?"

"Yes," replied the man.

"I presume they are also illuminated," said Mansur.

"Yes," said the man again.

"May I ask you a question now?" said Mansur.

"Certainly you may," replied the man.

"I do not know whether you have a daughter or not; but if you have one, and she — God will that it be not so! — was ugly, would you not paint her up a little in order to get her a husband?"

The man laughed and said: "What is the purpose of your questions?"

"It concerns your leather-bound illuminated book, and forgive me for so describing it, the painted daughter — the Koran. The book I offer you needs no decoration. It is beautiful in itself; it is the beautiful Word of God."

It was done so nicely that no offence was taken, and Mansur's parting with the group was amicable.

On one occasion he was arrested for selling — hawking would probably be the proper word — the Christian Scriptures in a public place, and taken to the police station at Shiraz. The police-chief was a Baha'i, and when he saw the Gospel portions Mansur was selling and discovered the pittance he was charging for them, he threw them aside scornfully and said, "Do you call that cheap trash the Word of God? How much would you have to pay for the Glorious Koran, or the Most Holy Book of Baha'u'llah? You can't compare this trash with those!"

"Do you pay for that?" asked Mansur, pointing to the electric light that then lit the darkened room. Then, without waiting for an answer, he crossed to the window, drew back the curtains and let in the brilliant sunshine, and turning to the police-chief said: "You don't pay for that; God's gifts are free! My books are free — the pittance is for my food. It's man-made things that are bought at a price, and such are the books you mentioned." He was released.

While based on Shiraz, Mansur visited the village of Qalat, 30 miles away, and found there a number of people who were ready to hear and receive the Gospel. The schoolmaster and a land owner and his daughter asked for baptism. So in March Mr. Richards, accompanied by Mansur and several other Christians, went to Qalat and stayed some days. Mr. Richards writes of this visit: "Next morning Mansur got busy extracting teeth and vaccinating countless babies. To see him working is an unforgettable sight! He did all his work on the roof (village houses usually had flat roofs). I can see him now, standing on the edge of the roof, two men holding down the patient, whilst he drew the tooth, which was then waved aloft in triumph, and thrust under the nose of the victim as if to assure him that it really was out. Potassium permanganate was then supplied from a tea pot, and the patient's face was washed — presumably to restore him." It seems that the people did not object to Mansur's dentistry, but some raised a riot as a result of the fearless preaching. However, this only increased the religious interest, and before the missionaries left Qalat, the three believers were baptized. Some years later a beautiful little church building was erected in this mountain village.

Mr. Richards writes vividly of the treatment which Mansur sometimes experienced:

"The following story will illustrate the spirit of the man. A short time ago he went to a mountain village in the neighborhood of Shiraz. He had visited the place before and knew the character of the inhabitants. They, too, knew him, and the most bigoted among them feared him. He had been there a few days when a hostile mob went to the house in which he was staying, and dragging him out, proceeded to expel him from the village. Men beat him with fists and sticks, women spat at him, others subjected him to indignities which cannot be mentioned here, but not one word of reproach did he utter. In the crowd was a blind man beating the air wildly with his stick as he made futile attempts to strike Mansur. Suddenly he turned on his oppressors and reproached them saying: 'How selfish you all are, you have given vent to your feelings by striking me. Would you prevent a poor blind man from easing his feelings in the same way?' Then forcing his way through the crowd, he approached the blind man and, bending his head before him, he said: 'Strike brother, strike!' Then after several blows 'Strike harder, my brother, if that will quench the fire in thy heart!' A few days later I visited that village and was told the story by one who was present.

"On the plain a few miles away from Qalat there stands a fortified village called Guyium, entry into which was never allowed us. Mansur had made many attempts, but had never been allowed to enter. On one occasion as we went by he suddenly said to me: 'The people of Guyium are more civilized than are those of Qalat.' I remarked that I could not agree, for they had never shown any sign of anything but hostility, and they had certainly been rude and indeed rough in their dealings with him on more than one occasion. He agreed that was true, 'but,' he added, 'the old women don't spit at you there!' "

In April, 1930, Mansur started out on the road once more and visited C.M.S. stations in Yezd and Kerman. There (in company with the Rev. H. E. J. Biggs, he made a journey by lorry into Iranian Baluchistan, to a town where no evangelist had ever gone before. The police soon confiscated their boxes of books, but Mansur went out into the street and distributed widely a supply of his "seed" which he had carefully hidden away. People wanted to come to their room and visit them, but the police prevented them. So Mansur stood at the open window and sang Christian hymns with a loud voice. That night a workman managed to reach them, and they had a long talk with him by the light of a lantern, and Mansur "read" the Bible to him. The man said he would like to become a Christian. Next day they were forced to return to Kerman.

Finally, after an absence of more than a year, Mansur Sang returned to Meshed. It had been indeed a memorable missionary journey, in which he had made a complete circuit of northern and central Iran, and only God has a record of how much "seed" had been sown, and how many learned to know Christ. The bold and lovable sower had been welcomed and honored by many of his brethren, and it is not surprising that he confessed to a friend in Shiraz that he did not relish going back to Khorasan, for, said he, "A prophet has no honor in his own country."

Mansur was a great letter-writer. The fact that he could not use a pen himself did not deter him in the least from sending letters to his friends. Wherever he happened to be, he would find someone who could write, and to this scribe he would dictate long epistles. Frequently the scribes, chosen more for their inexpensiveness than for their proficiency, wrote a fearful and wonderful hand, which often puzzled Persian scholars who attempted to read the letters. But if anyone could be found who was able to decipher these documents, they proved to be very interesting. For Mansur always related in great detail what he had said and done, and what had happened to him in his travels. It was easy to recognize his letters, whatever the handwriting might be, for he was always very careful to make the sign of the cross at the top of the first page. He also attached his seal to his letters, with the cross and the words, "Christ's Slave Mansur."

And so the years passed for this intrepid soldier of Christ. His experiences formed a striking parallel to those of the Apostle Paul, which he recounted in writing to the church in Corinth: "On frequent journeys, in dangers from rivers, danger from robbers, danger from my own people, . . . danger in the city, danger in the wilderness, . . .; in toil and hardship, through many a sleepless night, in hunger and thirst, often without food, in cold and exposure." The debonair way in which Mansur met these adventures is illustrated by a recollection of the Reverend W. N. Wysham: "Mansur was telling me that once a gang of boys caught him on the outskirts of a town and pelted him with rocks. I said, 'At least, Mansur, you had scriptural authority for going to the next city as rapidly as possible. I suppose you made haste elsewhere.' He grinned as he replied, 'No, I went into town to the heart of the bazaar, for there rocks were scarce and the streets too crooked for the boys to maneuver. I was soon preaching to a crowd.' "

For some years it was known that Mansur had a bad heart. However, he continued to travel about the country, and led an active life almost to the end. His last journey from Meshed to Teheran was made in the winter, and on the way he suffered much from exposure. From that time he began to fail. He was taken to the mission hospital in Teheran, and those who inquired of the doctor what was wrong with Mansur were told that *everything* was wrong with him — he was like the old one-horse shay that finally went down in total collapse. He was sick in mind as well as in body, and suffered from deep depression. Once he complained to a friend about the way his thoughts were causing him to suffer. Day and night he had no rest. "If only I could stop thinking!" he said. After a time he became quiet, and the cloud that had hung over him seemed to pass away.

On March 13, 1936, his old friend Dr. Schuler went into the hospital to see him. Mansur was sitting up in bed looking very weary. When asked how he was feeling, he replied in a feeble voice that he was not comfortable. When Dr. Schuler asked how his spiritual condition was, he pulled himself up and replied that he was all right. Then he added, "Let that man fear death who has no faith." Dr. Schuler left his bedside, saying he would return after the evangelistic meeting which was to be held in the office of Merat, the steward of the hospital. When he came back an hour later, Mansur was dead. He had told an orderly a few hours before that he was going to die that night, and he did. Mansur's travels and labors were over.

The funeral service was held next day in the Evangelical Presbyterian Church of Teheran, where Mansur had so often worshiped in years gone by. In accordance with his request, the service was conducted by Dr. Sa'eed, the most famous of the Muslim converts of Iran, who had befriended Mansur. His body, worn out in the service of his Master, was buried in the Protestant cemetery at Akbarabad, near Teheran. His grave is marked by a simple stone, with a cross at the top, similar to the one on Mansur's seal, and under it is the inscription in Persian:

123

MANSUR SANG
SERVANT OF JESUS CHRIST
1869-1936

Mansur Sang was unique! He was so different from his fellows that he made an indelible impression on all who knew him. He had faults and weaknesses which have not been recorded in this narrative, but these were due almost entirely to his personal and religious background. His life as Hasan inevitably conditioned his life as Mansur Sang. He was sometimes moody, doubtless due to the severe buffeting of events in his early life. Yet he was usually happy and refreshingly childlike in his disposition. He was fanatical in his faith, but the history of Iranian Islam abounds in fanaticism. The peripatetic dervish has long been an Iranian institution; Mansur was frequently called "the Christian dervish." Some of those he encountered on his journeys thought he was "touched," but there was always a method in his "madness," and an unwavering passion to win others to Christ. Those who knew him well still have echoing in their souls his sonorous voice proclaiming in Persian "Jesus Christ the Lord." There is no doubt that God laid hold of this strange personality to preach the Gospel in Iran.

To use Paul's words: Mansur Sang — Stone the Conqueror — was more than conqueror through Him who loved and saved him.

11

Nasrullah, "Universal Peace"

The most wonderful miracle in the field of biology is the birth of a new human being, and in the spiritual sphere the outstanding miracle is when a human being, with all his earthly desires, instincts, weaknesses and powers, is born again and becomes a child of God.

How much more difficult and complicated does it become when a man has grown up surrounded by dogma, sincere beliefs plus superstition and prejudices, which hold him prisoner and deny him the right to question or investigate the religion into which he has been born! Such is the position of a Muslim. Islam is a very real brotherhood, an impregnable rampart where all those within are sure that they alone have the true religion, they only are in the right, with the result that self-righteousness and pride become ingrained. Can a man who has grown up in such an environment be born again? We have seen this miracle occur in the lives of the Muslims whose stories have already been told in this book. We see it again in the life of Mirza Nasrullah.

Mirza Nasrullah Solh-i-Koll lived in the city of Yezd which is situated in a dry region near the center of Iran. Long before he came in touch with Christians, the Spirit of God breathed divine discontent into his heart. In his youth he had studied Muslin theology, and he came to know too much about the doctrines of Islam. He simply could not believe that God was like the Allah portrayed by the theologians. So he turned to the Baha'is, of whom there were a considerable number in Yezd, hoping to find something that would satisfy his thirst for God. The Baha'is claimed that the ones whose coming has been foretold in various religions, the Christ of the Christians, the Mahdi of the Muslims, the Shah Bahram of the Zoroastrians, have all appeared in the person of Baha'u'llah. He is the greatest of the many "Manifestations" of God who have come into the world, he will heal mankind's divisions and will bring all men together in one family, and he will establish on earth the

"Most Great Peace" predicted by the ancient prophets. All this sounded very good to Mirza Nasrullah, and he became a Baha'i, and took as his family name Solh-i-Koll, which means Universal Peace. (In English his name is usually spelt Solhekol.) But Baha'ism, like Islam, failed to satisfy his intellectual and spiritual cravings, and he continued to seek for the true God.

In the year 1921 Solhekol was a teacher in a Zoroastrian primary school in Yezd. His eyes were troubling him, so one day he went for treatment to the hospital of the Church Missionary Society which was nearby. After he was treated by the doctor, a copy of the Gospel of Luke was presented to him. This he prized and kept in his breast pocket, and whenever he had a few spare moments he studied it. One day near the end of the spring term, as he was reading his little book during a recess period, he came to the last part of the ninth chapter. As he read verse 62 in which Jesus says, "No man having put his hand to the plough and looking back is fit for the Kingdom of God," he was deeply impressed, the words seemed to pierce his heart, and he there and then decided that he must become a Christian.

At that time there was no one in Yezd who was authorized to teach a convert and prepare him for baptism. What was Solhekol to do? Moreover, his wife, who was a Baha'i, was bitterly opposed to Christianity. He felt the only thing he could do was to go to Isfahan where there was a congregation of Christians, and where the bishop of the Anglican Church resided, and ask to be instructed and made ready for baptism. To Solhekol it was unthinkable that he should keep his new-found faith to himself and join the ranks of the "secret believers." But Isfahan was 260 miles away, and the only means of transportation available to him was his bicycle with worn-out tires. Not daunted by these difficulties, he sat down and wrote his resignation to the head of the school where he taught. He also wrote a farewell note to his wife, telling her why he was going to Isfahan, and another to one of the women missionaries, asking her to look after his wife and child (then very ill). He also wrote to several friends explaining what he had done. Truly he burned his bridges behind him.

Then with eight tomans (about $8 in these days) in his pocket, and a bicycle repair kit, Solhekol set out on his journey. At that time roads were only tracks across the desert, stony, rough, and deeply rutted with sand, very difficult to negotiate with a bicycle. After a very short time the tires wore out completely and even the repair kit proved of no avail. Sadly Solhekol pushed his bike to the next town, some miles away, where he waited in the home of a friend, hoping that he might get a ride to Isfahan. Then a truck came along bound for Yezd, and he felt that God was guiding him to return home, and to set out again for Isfahan. He got back four days later, covered with dust and utterly worn out.

In the meantime, his Baha'i wife had come weeping to Miss Nouhie Aiden, one of the missionaries, saying that she did not believe a word of Solhekol's letter to her, and that he had evidently gone to Isfahan to enjoy himself, and perhaps to marry another wife. Miss Aiden assured her that as a Christian he could not do that, and would be a much better husband to her than he had been before.

After he put his hand to the plough, there was for Solhekol no turning back. He lost no time in buying himself some new tires, and in spite of all persuasion, pleading and ridicule from friends and neighbors, he started off again. Miss Aiden took the precaution of sending a telegram to Bishop Linton in Isfahan, asking him to receive the traveller when he arrived, for she feared that if without warning they saw his dusty figure suddenly appearing, worn out after a long journey by bicycle, they might think he was a little mad. He arrived safely, and was welcomed by the bishop, who arranged for him to be taught and baptized. He was away from home for three months.

During Solhekol's absence the baby boy, who had been very ill when he went away, became rapidly worse. Late one night Fatemeh Jan, the child's mother, came to see Miss Aiden, saying that she was afraid he would die that night. And since her husband had given strict instructions that he should be baptized, she asked that this be done at once. So about midnight, by candlelight on the veranda, Dr. Lucy Maloy and two other missionaries baptized him. A strange baptism indeed, the father of the child not yet baptized himself, and the mother violently opposed, but superstitiously afraid not to carry out her husband's orders! Soon after, the baby died.

After his baptism in Isfahan, Solhekol returned to Yezd. The head of the school in which he taught was quite convinced that he had gone to Isfahan to get a more highly paid job in the Stuart Memorial College of the Mission. However, he agreed to take him back, and Solhekol resumed his work at the school at the same salary. But life was now not easy for him. By becoming a Christian he raised up a great many enemies for himself. Having changed from Islam to Baha'ism and then to Christianity, he was accused of being a fickle time-server. A group of friends came to see him one day, and after the customary polite interchange of courtesies, one of them said, "Now Mirza Nasrullah, tell us what happened to you! Why this extraordinary trip to Isfahan, and what's all this about your becoming a Christian?"

After a short pause Solhekol replied, "You will agree with me that men do things from different motives. Most people aim at getting wealth, but you see that my trip to Isfahan cost me new tires for my bicycle and expenses while there, and now I am back at work in my old job. So money can hardly have been the incentive. Others do things to get fame and approbation, but I have only succeeded in getting myself known as a crazy fool. Lastly, people do things for God. I leave it to you to decide whether that could have been the reason for my going." Nobody really believed that he had become a Christian. There must have been some other reason for his journey, they said.

At home, for two people so unequally yoked together, things were far from easy. Fatemeh Jan had expressed her fear that her husband would now force her to become a Christian. But her missionary friends explained to her that neither he nor anyone else would do this, and if she should ever herself wish to become a Christian, she would have to plead to be accepted. So Solhekol never discussed religion with his wife, never asked her to read the Gospels or to attend the women's Bible class. However, he used to leave his Bible and other books he was reading on a shelf, and he said he was quite sure they were being read. His name meant "Peace," and he was indeed a peaceable person, but he had much to contend with. If Christians came to see him, he would often find that his wife had locked up the tea and sugar and gone out. She made life as difficult for him as she could, but he never suggested divorce, and never thought of taking a second wife, which he would probably have done in such a situation had he been a Muslim or a Baha'i.

As the days went on, Solhekol tried to show by his courtesy and gentleness and understanding something of the love and joy he had found in Christ. And then after eight years Fatemeh Jan by her own decision became a Christian and asked for baptism. During those years a fine healthy boy and two girls had been born to them, and it was a wonderful day when the mother, radiantly happy, was baptized with her children.

After some years Solhekol gave up his position as teacher in the Zoroastrian school and served in the church, first as an evangelist, and then after his ordination, as a pastor in Yezd and Kerman.

Once when Solhekol attended an inter-church conference in Teheran, he was deeply impressed by lectures given by Mrs. A. C. Boyce on the Christian home, and when he returned to

Yezd he tried to carry out his new ideas in his own home. He got from the Inter-Mission Literature Committee in Teheran large colored pictures of children asking a blessing before the meal, children playing together and kneeling for prayer at night. They always had short family prayers in the home each day.

One day Solhekol mentioned to a friend that he and his wife couldn't manage to keep candy or cakes in the house, as the children always ate them up! His friend said, "That's simple, lock them up!" "Yes," said the father thoughtfully, "that would do, but then we don't have any locks or keys in the house!" The children grew up unrepressed and happy, but also courteous and obedient.

Solhekol was often away from home on his evangelistic trips, taking with him his "Magic Lantern" (a projector operated by a kerosene lamp), with which he showed pictures of the life of Christ in the villages to eager audiences of Muslims and Zoroastrians. He and his wife had a pact that on his return from these journeys to his home, the first evening was to be given up entirely to the enjoyment and happiness of being together again. No mention of financial or other difficulties was to mar the family happiness that evening. Next morning was quite time enough to go into problems and do the accounts.

Due to the enthusiasm of the Reverend R. N. Sharp, pastor of the Anglican Church in Yezd, a bookshop for the sale of Christian literature and other books was opened on the main avenue of Yezd, and Solhekol was in charge of this for certain hours of the day. The hope had been that this shop might become a Christian reading room, but because of the difficulties involved in securing a permit from the local government, it was decided to continue as a shop for the sale of books. Then the official was asked, "Could the bookshop manager have a desk and a chair?" "Most certainly," was the reply. "And could there be a chair for the customer?" "Yes," said the official, "that also would be all right." So, with the law on his side, Solhekol would sit on the corner of the desk while two customers used the chairs, and together they would discuss Christian books. "This is much better than talking to a large crowd," the manager explained.

To the east of Iran lies Afghanistan, a country which had long been closed to the entrance of Christian missionaries. Many had attempted to enter but without success, and for more than a century much prayer had been offered that the Gospel might be made known to the millions of Muslims in that land. As Solhekol considered the situation, he felt that God was calling him to help meet this need, and he asked to be allowed to go to Afghanistan for an evangelistic tour. He complained that the church in Iran had not yet sent any missionaries to work outside their own country, and he would like to be the first foreign missionary to go from Iran. No doubt he remembered that in ancient times missionaries from Iran had carried the Gospel all across Asia to China, and why should they not do so once more? When it was pointed out that Afganistan did not permit missionaries to enter, and that if he went he might be murdered, he replied, "Then I would be the church's first martyr! I would like that." So he was given permission to try to get a passport, but all his efforts proved futile. However, he learned that peddlers from Iran often crossed the border without formal visas, sold their wares, and returned home without any difficulty. He decided to go as a peddler, taking tea and sugar, spices and cakes, beautiful embroidered table cloths made at the Garden of Arts in the Mission in Isfahan, and other odds and ends for which he might find a market. He also took some Gospels and tracts, and set off alone for Meshed, in northeast Iran.

One of the missionaries in Meshed wrote thus of Solhekol's coming to that city: "When this quiet little man arrived in Meshed on his way to Herat in Afghanistan, we had the privilege of entertaining him. It was indeed a dangerous undertaking on which he had embarked, and he well realized this. Before going on his way eastward, he asked to receive the communion, and we had a simple service in our home. While he was in Afghanistan he was remembered in our prayers, and he received a warm welcome on his safe return to Meshed. He told us that he was determined not to carry back with him the Christian literature he had been unable to distribute, so he used the pages to wrap up small portions of tea and sugar and spices, confident that some people would read them. Also, on the night before his departure from Herat he had divided his own copy of the Persian Bible into a number of small portions, and in the darkness had gone about the streets leaving the portions in numerous places, and then had hastily left the city. He had no difficulty crossing the border, either going or returning. And since the language in that part of Afghanistan is Persian, he had no trouble in making himself understood. Whether anything had been accomplished by this courageous entrance into the 'closed land' we did not know. But Solhekol must be remembered as one of those who in obedience to Christ's command have risked their lives in order to make an entrance for the Gospel in Afghanistan."

Solhekol was a great reader and a lover of books. He did not know much English, but he knew both Persian and Arabic very well, and he translated several Arabic books into Persian.

The most important of these is a book called *The King of Love,* written in Arabic by Miss Constance Padwick. It is a life of Christ in ordinary language. For the Persian edition Solhekol wrote an introduction which is charming. He mentions the well-known Persian legends of Rustam and Sohrab, Amir Arsalan, etc., and says he has a better story to tell, and what's more it's true. How nice it would be if he could drop in on his readers for an evening and tell them his true story, instead of these wonder tales they listen to! However, as this cannot be, he will send out his book instead, and hopes everyone will enjoy it. And then he tells the story of Jesus Christ. This book has been widely read in Iran.

It was the belief of Solhekol, as of some other Christians, that one of the best ways to prepare the way for the Gospel would be to translate and publish the Koran in Persian. Few of the people in Iran know enough Arabic to understand the Koran, and at that time the Muslim authorities were unwilling for it to be translated, since Arabic is the language, they say, in which God spoke to Mohammed. Hence, most Muslims were quite ignorant of its contents. Solhekol was sure that after understanding the Koran, people would want to read and believe the Bible.

In Iran the authorities have usually been very suspicious of any kind of foreign political propaganda. Once when Solhekol was making a tour of the villages round about Yezd, showing religious slides with his "Magic Lantern," the local officials thought that this instrument must be for broadcasting or transmitting political propaganda. So they marched him off to prison. He assured them that the lantern was only for showing pictures, and offered to give them a show in the prison. This was acceptable, and in the evening he showed them the pictures of the life of Christ, with officers and prisoners present. He had to spend the night locked in a filthy room with all the other prisoners. In the morning when he was set free, he first asked for a broom and water, and himself cleaned the dirty prison room.

After a severe illness in Kerman which affected his heart, Solhekol retired from active service in the church, and settled in Yezd. He died quite suddenly of a heart attack on May 12, 1955. At that time there was no ordained minister of the church in Yezd to conduct a Christian funeral service, but his faithful wife took a firm stand that he should have a Christian burial. There were both Muslims and Baha'is who would have liked to carry off the body of the deceased, and claim him for themselves, but they were not permitted to do so. A young Christian weaver very bravely came forward and undertook the arrangements for getting a grave dug and transporting the coffin, and he reverently read the burial service. This was a courageous thing to do in a bigoted place like Yezd, and might have brought the young Christian much persecution and danger. The service was a clear witness to the power and hope of Christ.

In a letter found on Solhekol's desk after his death, addressed to a friend, he says, "The Church of Jesus will grow through the suffering of the Iranian people." Every Christian has to suffer for his faith. Many are cast out of their homes, and cut off from their friends. They stand the risk of physical persecution and of being turned out of their jobs. Each convert is a miracle of the Risen Lord. The church truly grows through the suffering of the Iranian people.

12

Jalily, Man of God

Three friends traveled from Teheran to Isfahan to attend a gathering of Christians. While there they visited some of the beautiful and historic buildings of the city, famous throughout the world for its mosques and minarets. Since the Shi'ite Muslims considered the non-Muslims to be unclean, it was usually impossible for Christians to enter the mosques in Iran. However, some of the finest of the Isfahan mosques were no longer used for worship, and tourists of all religions were permitted to enter them. So to the great Mesjid-i-Shah (the Shah's Mosque) came the three Christians. After admiring the exquisite tile work, made by skilled artisans more than three centuries ago, they walked to a central spot under the huge dome to hear the famous echo. The first two men whistled and shouted, and then listened to their voices again and again and again, as the repeated echoes brought them back from the heights above. Then the third member of the party, a little man with a gentle voice, stepped up to the speaking point, and looking up into the vast dome opened wide his mouth and shouted with all his might in the Persian language, "Jesus Christ the Lord, Jesus Christ the Lord!"

Who was this bold Christian who proclaimed his faith in a place where the Muslim creed had been sounded forth ten thousand times, but where the Lordship of Jesus Christ had never before been announced? It was not the American missionary or the Hebrew Christian but the Muslim convert Mahmud Jalily, who until a few years previously would have joined heartily in repeating the creed of Islam, "There is no God except Allah, and Mohammed is the Apostle of Allah." What had happened to change a devout Muslim into a radiant and fearless Christian?

Mahmud was born in Tabriz in 1882 A.D., and his mother tongue was Turkish. When he was six years of age his father took the family to Teheran, and there they remained. The father

133

was a *vazir* (minister) to the wife of the Shah, and Mahmud was reared in the Royal Court. Since he was an only child, his father was devoted to him, kept him at his side when he was at home, and took him with him on his various journeys. Instead of sending his beloved son to school, the father employed teachers to come to the women's quarters of the Court to instruct Mahmud. He was taught Persian and Arabic and French, and received what was then considered a liberal education, including music (the playing of the *tar*).

When the boy became a youth he began to serve in the Royal Court and there had the opportunity to associate with the chief people of the Kingdom. During the reign of Mozaffar-ed-Din Shah (1896-1907), Mahmud's father died, and the young man was given a position in the Office of Finance. It was in the latter part of the reign of this Shah that the enlightened people of Iran demanded a constitution, and there was a bitter struggle between the Constitutionalists and the Monarchy. In this conflict young Jalily sided with the Constitutionalists and took an active part in the revolution which gave Iran for the first time a constitution and a parliament. With the idealism of youth, Jalily was overjoyed at this victory, and thought that all his problems and those of his beloved Iran had been solved. "But," said he in later years, "I soon saw that I was many miles from my purpose and desire."

Jalily married, and became the father of several sons and daughters. He had a good position in the government mint, and enjoyed the respect of his acquaintances. However, these things, like the granting of the constitution, failed to satisfy him. He saw in himself no peace and no assurance for the future. His wife died, and after a time he married again and had three more sons. He was transferred from the mint to the Ministry of Finance, where he was given a good position. But his heart was not at rest. Once he went with a group of devout Muslims to the sacred city of Qum, and there spent some days in prayer and fasting. Often in Teheran he would rise very early, leave his home in Jalilabad (which was named for his father), and walk to the city gate. Then outside the city in the solitude of the desert he would pray that God would guide him and supply the thing that was lacking in his life, whatever it was. And so the years passed.

Finally the idea occurred to Jalily that perhaps his need was for a more modern education. He should learn English, read new books, and associate with educated men, and perhaps he would find more meaning in life. So he made inquiries and found an English teacher who would come to his home and give him private lessons. The teacher was a student in the school of the Presbyterian Mission in Teheran. His name was Ahmad, son of the sister of Nozad. (See Chapter 5.) Through his uncle, Ahmad had become a Christian, but Jalily did not at first know this. What he noticed at once was the fine character of his teacher. Ahmad was courteous and truthful and kind. He was also an excellent teacher, and before long Jalily was able to speak and to read a little in this difficult foreign tongue, which Ahmad had learned so well in the mission school.

The youngest of Jalily's sons by his first wife was Jahangir, and he was greatly loved by his father. Seeing in Ahmad a sample of the education given by Dr. Samuel Jordan and his colleagues in Alborz College, Jalily began to feel that this was what he wanted for Jahangir. So in due time the son became a pupil in the Christian school. There he learned English, and there he came to know Jesus Christ. But he did not tell his father that he wanted to become a Christian.

In November, 1930, the little Evangelical (Presbyterian) church in Teheran did something that was unprecedented in Iran. Every night for a week evangelistic meetings were conducted in the mission chapel, for the purpose of making Christ known to the Muslims of the city. Some feared that such a bold attempt to convert Muslims in a land where the official religion was Islam would do harm rather than good, and might even result in the expulsion of the missionaries. But the church resolved to go forward in faith. Invitation cards were printed, inviting people to attend a series of addresses in the chapel of the mission, to be given by a speaker from another city. Much prayer was offered. The meetings were held as planned. Every night the chapel was crowded with eager listeners, both Christians and non-Christians. And the effort met with no serious opposition.

When Jahangir Jalily came home from school one day he brought with him an invitation card. "My father," he said, "our principal, Dr. Jordan, sends you his greetings, and with them this card, inviting you to the church tonight to hear an address." Jalily had never been to a church, but he had often attended lectures of various sorts in other places in order to increase his knowledge. Therefore, since the famous Dr. Jordan had invited him, and since his son was eager for him to go, Jalily decided to accept. That night he and Jahangir went together to the chapel in Ghavam-us-Saltaneh Avenue. Jalily was expecting to hear a lecture on some secular subject.

As he entered the well-filled auditorium and glanced at the people seated there, he felt quite superior to them — for had not he been reared in the Court of the Shah? Then he and his son sat down in the middle of the crowd, and the meeting began. Soon Jalily reaized that this was not the kind of gathering he had supposed it to be. This was a religious meeting! The singing pleased him, and he tried without much success to follow the strange tunes. He was quieted by the prayers, spoken not in Arabic like the Muslim worship, but in Persian. And then the address began. The speaker described how Adam, the father of the human race, had disobeyed God, and by doing so had involved both himself and all mankind in sin and death. And then he told how God had promised a Savior, born of a woman, who would defeat Satan. And he explained how this Savior, born of the Virgin Mary, had died on the cross and risen from the dead to deliver men from sin and death. He closed with an invitation to his hearers to believe on Jesus Christ and be saved.

As Jalily listened to the message he was deeply moved. "All the events of my life," said he later, "passed before my eyes like a moving picture, and as I gazed on my past deeds I saw myself condemned. I had been like a blind man. Then when my eyes were opened I saw all the filthiness of my life." Jalily had lived a good moral life, and was indeed better than most men. But suddenly in that hour God opened his eyes, and for the first time in his life he saw himself as God saw him, a sinner needing a Savior. And he heard and heeded the Savior's invitation, "Come unto me and I will give you rest!"

The meeting ended, the crowds went out, and a number of men remained to learn more of Christ, among them Jalily and his son. The speaker explained to this group of inquirers that as a sick man goes to a doctor whom he trusts and commits himself to his care, so we who are afflicted with the deadly disease of sin may go to the great physician, Jesus Christ. He loved us and died for us, and he conquered death and is alive with us today. He is ready to receive and forgive and save all those who trust themselves to him. Then the speaker asked who wanted to come to the Savior.

Several men arose and spoke. Jalily and Jahangir also stood up, and with trembling voice the father said, "When I entered this room I thought I was the best man here. But now I know there was no greater sinner in the meeting than I. I believe on Jesus Christ as my Savior, and I will follow him as long as I live."

Later Jalily said, "I do not know how it was possible for me to confess before those people that I was a bad man, for all my life I had tried to make people believe I was a good man. Truly an unseen power lifted me to my feet and enabled me to confess my sins. When I did so, at that very momvent I experienced in myself joy such as one would have who was relieved of a

136

heavy burden. I felt that I was no longer my former self, I was a new being. On that night I was born again! That troubled heart found quiet, that self-esteem was changed to humility, that enmity to friendliness. Instead of avoiding people I wanted to come near them. For me the world became new. I had found what I had so long sought."

When father and son returned to their home, Khanum Jalily at once noticed the change in her husband. "Why are you so happy tonight," she demanded, "have you been drinking?"

"No," exclaimed Jalily, "you know I do not drink — I have become a Christian!"

Jahangir was very happy over his father's decision, but other members of the family were not. They felt that Jalily had disgraced them by giving up their national faith, and adopting the religion of the foreigners. But the father endured their taunts with patience and humility, and the love of Christ prevailed. Later his wife and the younger members of his family also became Christians.

Of these meetings in which Jalily and others were converted, Mrs. Arthur C. Boyce of the Presbyterian Mission wrote thus to her friends in America: "The meetings were for both men and women but the men far outnumbered the women, except on Wednesday when only ladies were admitted. . . . Invitations were given by means of small printed cards with the date filled in by hand. Three thousand of these cards were given out during the week (and the church was well filled at each meeting, from 200 to 250 being present. . . . Although most of those present were Muslims, Islam was ignored. The preacher might have been talking to a church full of people at home, showing how we all need a savior from sin, and strength to lead a life which is pure and a life of love. The response was wonderful; it seemed that men had just been waiting for this opportunity. All who wished to know more, or who wanted this new life, were asked to remain after the service. From thirty to forty stayed every night and in the presence of such a number many said they wanted to be Christians, or they accepted Christ, or asked to be prayed for. At the close of these eight meetings sixty had signified their desire to be Christians. Most of these are young men, twenty from the (mission) college and about as many from the Jewish school (of the Anglican church) and the rest from outside. . . . We wonder if such a series of meetings with like results was ever held in any Muslim land before. Do you wonder that we feel that a new era of direct evangelistic work is before us, and that we thank God and take courage?" Sad to say, many of those sixty who began the race so enthusiastically soon fell by the wayside. But Jalily did not.

137

In a hostile environment, and especially in a Muslim land, many believers are sorely tempted to keep their faith to themselves and to "put their lamps under a bushel," lest they cause trouble for themselves or their families. But Jalily was as unable to keep silence as were the apostles in Jerusalem when the rulers forbade them to preach. The day after his great decision Jalily went to his office and there told his friends that he had become a Christian. He invited them to come to his home, that he might tell them why he had done this. One night they came in a body and he gave his testimony to Christ's salvation. Some were impressed, and some opposed him. He soon formed the habit of bowing in prayer for a few moments when he first sat down at his office desk each morning, and those who were displeased with him took this opportunity of annoying him by calling him and interrupting his prayer. In patience he endured this petty persecution for Christ's sake. But his superiors in the Ministry of Finance never threatened to dismiss him because he had given up Islam. They needed the services of a reliable man like Jalily, and he was retained.

After his conversion Jalily began to study the New Testament, with which he had no previous acquaintance, and ever after his chief joy was poring over the Word of God. After nine months he and two other converts from Islam received Christian baptism on August 27, 1931, in a conference in Teheran at which members of the Anglican and Presbyterian churches in Iran were present. Soon after this the three new believers formed a little brotherhood to strengthen their own faith and to give the Good News of salvation to others. Once a week on Monday nights they would invite their friends to the home of Jalily, and there he would with perfect Iranian courtesy serve tea with his own hands to his guests. Then he would read the Bible to them, and tell them what Christ had done for him and would do for them, if they only believed on the Savior. These meetings in Jalily's home continued for 35 years, and in them many men met Christ face to face.

Usually the spirit in these informal gatherings was warm and friendly, for Jalily was always more eager to preach Christ than to attack Islam. But there were times when enemies invaded his home, and did all in their power to break up his meetings. Once when the famous author Lotfi Levonian from Beirut was a guest in the meeting, some rude opponents of the Gospel created a difficult situation. A Christian army officer who was present and who had been a champion boxer, exerted his influence to protect the honored guest from harm and became his body guard as he walked home! Professor Levonian never forgot that night in Jalily's home.

As the room in which the meetings were held had become too small to accommodate the guests, Jalily went to considerable expense and built a larger room, with a window opening on the street, that passersby might hear and see and come in.

Not content with inviting friends to his home, Jalily began to go into the streets with Christian books and tracts in his hands, selling Scriptures and Christian literature, and inviting men who showed interest to come to the Christian reading room and services of the church. In Iran an educated man would think it was beneath his dignity to become a peddler of books on the streets. But for Jalily it was an honor to witness thus to his Lord. Whatever his old friends might say, he must be faithful to his new friend, Jesus Christ. His utter sincerity and humility disarmed any who might have been offended by his courageous presentation of the Gospel, and often those who were at first opposed became friends.

Every evening an informal class for the study of the Bible was conducted in the reading room at the Presbyterian Mission, to which both Christians and Muslims were welcomed. Jalily became a regular member, and later a leader of the group, and here he found many opportunities for telling the young men who gathered there what Christ had done for him. In this class, which continued for many years, a number of Muslim men came to know the Savior.

The path of a convert is never a smooth one, and Jalily's life as a Christian was not without its problems. Though his wife had become a Christian, a situation arose which led Jalily, at the insistence of his Muslim relatives, to resort to divorce. Then a dark cloud descended on his home. One day a Christian brother, Mansur Sang (see Chapter 10)), came to see Jalily, and as they knelt in prayer, Mansur said, "You are a Christian. As God has forgiven you, you must forgive her. Bring her back to your home!" Jalily felt that this was a command from the Lord, and obeyed. Later the couple were reunited in Christian marriage in a private service in the church.

In a letter in August 1938, a missionary in Teheran wrote as follows about Jalily: "If ever a man was truly converted and born again, Jalily was. During the past eight years he has been a wonderful example of what Christ can do for a Muslim. He holds a good position in public office, where he is trusted and respected. But his purpose and joy in life is to serve Christ and the Church. He is an honored elder, and a leader in the evangelistic work of the church, and I have never heard anyone question the reality of his Christian faith and life. He is indeed an Iranian saint! He has been sorely tried, and has shown the love of Christ to a degree rarely seen among Christians anywhere. What a constant joy and blessing this good man is to all of us!

"But while the father has been growing steadily into the likeness of Christ, the son who brought him to the church that night (eight years ago) has been drifting farther and farther away. He was a gifted fellow, and has great ambition. He loved Christ, but he realized that if he was baptized and made a public confession of faith, he would not be able to attain the heights to which he aspired. And so he had tried to hold to Christ with one hand, and to the world with the other. . . . He refused baptism, stopped attending church, and gave his whole attention to getting on in the world. He wrote a book which attracted some notice, and he secured a good position. But his father grieved much for him, for he had gone into the far country.

"Then suddenly last week he returned! I saw the father in our mission hospital and he said, 'My son has just returned from a journey and he is very ill. I have come to take the doctor to see him!' When the doctor came back he told me he feared it was a serious matter. As soon as I could I went with the father to call on him in the home of his sister where he was staying. I was shocked to see how thin and weak the poor fellow had become. But he gave me a smiling welcome and as soon as I had sat down beside him, he said, 'I am very weak, both in body and in spirit. I need help!' I needed to ask no questions, for that one word made it perfectly clear to me that the prodigal had set his face toward home! I assured him of God's forgiveness, and reminded him of the blood of God's Son which cleanseth us from all sin. I bade him cast his burdens at Christ's feet, and find rest for his soul. And then we prayed, he and his father and I. . . .

"Two days later I called again. The sick man was better . . . and told me of his resolve to return to the church as soon as he was well enough, and be baptized, and take an active part in all the work of the church. 'How much it means to one to be with Christian brothers,' he said, 'and to work with them in the service of God!' "

But Jahangir Jalily never again had the opportunity which he so much desired to serve God in the church. He grew weaker and weaker and in the spring of 1939 he died, trusting in Christ. Of his death a friend wrote, "It was very sad, for he had great ability as a writer, and might have rendered large service with his pen to the cause of Christ in Iran. The members of his family were heartbroken, but the father bore this sorrow with that amazing quietness and trust which only Christ can give."

Eager to devote all his time and strength to the service of his Master, Jalily at the age of sixty made a request of the Ministry of Finance, in which he had served for many years, that he be retired. His request was granted, and he was given a pension. Now he was free to spend more time in the reading room talking to inquirers, and in the streets selling Christian literature. He also frequently accompanied evangelists as they made journeys to the provincial cities. As the missionaries went from one government office to another to meet the Muslim officials and sell Christian books to them, it frequently happened that the officials knew Jalily or his sons, and they always welcomed him with courtesy and usually bought supplies of his books. In these visits he never failed to give his testimony to Jesus Christ, his Lord. Though Muslims often show resentment when Christians refer to their Savior as "Son of God," a term which the Koran vigorously rejects, Jalily always seemed to glory in calling Christ "God's only Son," and sensing his deep sincerity, his hearers seldom objected.

During this period Jalily became one of the trusted leaders in the Evangelical (Presbyterian) Church of Iran. In Teheran he often spoke from the pulpit, especially in the Sunday evening evangelistic services. He was not a brilliant preacher, but his earnestness and utter devotion to Christ always impressed his hearers. The evangelistic committee invited him to become a lay evangelist. He joyfully accepted this position, and continued his efforts to give the Good News of Salvation to his fellow countrymen.

Jahangir's sister was deeply devoted to him, and at the time of his last illness professed her faith in Christ. But she did not ask for baptism, and in the eight years that followed she showed no real interest in becoming a Christian. All this time her father prayed for her. Then in April, 1947, her father's prayers were answered. Of this a missionary writes as follows:

"The married daughter of Aqa Jalily, the saintly evangelist of the church .... came to see me one morning and said she wanted to become a Christian. She confessed that she had not been pleased when her father became a Christian sixteen years ago, and she had often spoken unkindly about him. But a short time ago, she had seen something that had completely changed her attitude. Someone in her presence talked very badly to her father, and said many unkind and untrue things about him. But he had borne it all with Christlike patience and humility, and never said a word in reply.

" 'That was too much for me,' said the daughter, 'for I had never seen so noble a spirit as that. My father is poor, I am wealthy and have all that one could desire — but I don't have my father's patience and forgiveness. I am not happy and I want what he has. So I have come to you to ask you to lead me to Christ, to put my hand in His hand, that I may become like my dear father!' For an hour we talked of Christ, and her father, and as the tears flowed down her face, she confessed her sinfulness, prayed to God for forgiveness and yielded her life to Christ. It was the story of the prodigal all over again, except that this time it was a daughter instead of a son who returned to the Father." Jalily was radiantly happy that his daughter had come to Christ. Mehri Khanum was baptized, and served Christ joyfully and faithfully till her death a few years later.

An older brother of Jahangir, Abdollah Jalily, was a highly respected teacher of French in Teheran. One morning he arose early to go to an appointment, and as he was crossing the street, he was hit by a car and killed. Since he was a Muslim, his body was taken at once to the mosque for the funeral service. Someone came to Jalily and said, "Please come at once with me to the mosque." Not knowing why he should go, but sensing that something serious had happened, he entered the mosque and found many people assembled there. Then he was told that this was the funeral of his son Abdollah. The father was overcome with grief. How could he endure such a sudden and such a cruel blow? Then there came to him the words, "Let not not your heart be troubled, believe in God, believe also in me! Come unto me . . . and I will give you rest." He looked to Christ, and found such peace and strength that all who saw him were amazed at his composure. A few days later a memorial service for Abdollah Jalily was held in the hall of the Ministry of Education, and the bereaved father was one of those who spoke, giving his testimony as a Christian to a large number of his son's friends and colleagues. When he had finished the Minister of Education, a Muslim, rose and said, "This man is a man of faith, and that is why he is so greatly sustained in this sorrow." In after years Jalily often referred to this experience as an example of what Christ had meant to him in his many great sorrows.

The Synod of the Evangelical Church appointed a committee to arrange a training program for evangelists, and in the summer of 1948 a number of men and women spent four months in the Garden of Evangelism at the foot of the Alborz Mountains, ten miles north of Teheran, in study and prayer and preparation for the task of evangelizing Iran. The training was continued in succeeding summers and in 1950 the first class of seven graduates, one of whom was Jalily, received their certificates.

Jalily was the oldest and one of the most enthusiastic of the students in this school. He worked hard and memorized Bible verses as faithfully as did the younger students. It was with difficulty that he was restrained from sweeping the dining room and carrying buckets of water to the kitchen. To him it was truly heaven to be in the happy fellowship of the Garden, and his presence was a blessing to everyone. One day Jalily's daughter came to the Garden to say goodbye before leaving for America to see her son, who was a student in California. She stood by her father, and with tears streaming down her cheeks, told how his holy life had led her to Christ. All were deeply moved.

In the same year in which he was graduated, Jalily had the privilege of returning to the city of Tabriz, which he had not seen since his childhood. There in his birthplace he gave his testimony to the reality of his new birth in Christ. Also while there he wrote and published at his own expense a Persian booklet entitled, "Glad Tidings of Salvation." In this he described his early life, his conversion, and his service as a Christian. He closed his account with this sentence: "I thank God that I have had this opportunity to come to the city of my birth and give the Good News of Jesus Christ by means of His Word to my dear fellow citizens. Mahmud Jalily."

While in Tabriz Jalily eagerly sought out his relatives in the hope that he might lead them to Christ, but they did not welcome their cousin who had become an infidel! However, a young doctor and others in Tabriz were drawn to Jalily by his loving spirit, and through him to Christ.

North of the Alborz Mountains lies the great province of Mazanderan, which stretches for many miles along the southern shores of the Caspian Sea. No permanent mission station had ever been located in this region, though a number of missionary journeys had been made to several of the larger towns by evangelists and doctors from Teheran. Mazanderan became Jalily's special concern. Again and again, either alone or in company with one or more of his Christian brothers, he visited the cities of this province. Usually the officials treated the gracious evangelist with courtesy and respect, and he became well known throughout the province. It was amazing how high school students were attracted to this elderly man. As soon as Jalily would arrive in town, flocks of boys would visit his room in the hotel and listen eagerly to his message of Jesus Christ.

A missionary wrote as follows about Jalily's work in Mazanderan: "I went to the Caspian coast, travelling by bus over the very high mountains which separate the plateau from the sea. The scenery is indeed magnificent, and the precipices are terrific. I joined Jalily in Babul, the chief city of the province, just as he was about to return to Teheran after spending his vacation there with his wife (a vacation for him is doing evangelistic work!). He was seated in the bus about to leave when I unexpectedly appeared at the door. Immediately he got out, leaving his wife to go back to Teheran with the baggage, and stayed behind to help me, without even a tooth brush! How thankful I was that he did so, for he is known and loved by many people in this city, to which he has so often journeyed to sell books and to tell men of Christ, and through him I was able to meet many friends.

"The next day a great event occurred. Several years ago a high school student in Babul had told Jalily that he wanted to become a Christian. He brought a friend, and they brought others, till now we have the names of over 100 students in this one government school who have expressed a desire to become Christians. There was no one to give them regular instruction, and doubtless many of them understood very little of what it meant to become a Christian, but never in any other school in Iran, not even in our former mission schools, did so many Muslim boys ever say that they wanted to become Christians. It seemed best to delay the baptism of these boys till the sincerity of their faith had been proved, and so none were baptized till yesterday.

"Would that you could have looked in on the little service held around the table in a room in Babul yesterday afternoon, when the first two of these Christian young men were baptized! They had fearleslsy professed their faith before their families and their schoolmates, they had each led a number of their friends to accept Christ, they had waited three years for baptism — and in the presence of their French teacher, a Catholic, and of the evangelists Jalily and Nikpur, I had the great joy of receiving them into the church of Jesus Christ. Then we partook of the Lord's Supper together, the Catholic gladly communing with us. These young soldiers of Christ are confident that in a short time there will be many others ready for baptism, and with God's blessing there will soon be a church in Mazanderan. Last night there were at least 20 men in my room in the hotel, eagerly listening as Aqa Jalily told them of the new life he had received from Christ, and most of them openly said that they believed in Christ."

So promising was the situation in Mazanderan that the Board of Evangelism of the Synod decided to undertake permanent work there, and in 1949 Jalily and his wife gladly agreed to leave their home and children in Teheran for a time and join the Reverend and Mrs. C. H. Allen of the Presbyterian Mission, in order to establish in Babul the "Mazanderan Mission." Rooms were rented and nicely fixed up for a reading room, a class room and a place of worship. Many young men began to come to this center, and a number were given systematic Bible instruction by Mr. Allen, in preparation for baptism. Church services were conducted every Sunday. Visits were made to other cities to encourage the little groups of Christians and to evangelize Muslims. Hopes were high that many people in Mazanderan would believe and that churches would soon be established in the different cities.

Sad to say, these hopes were not realized. Because of the political situation, the Allens were forced to leave Babul. It was not possible for the Jalilys to remain longer away from their Teheran home. And since no other experienced Iranian evangelist was available, the Board of Evangelism with great reluctance voted at the end of 1951 to discontinue the "Mazanderan Mission." When this decision was anounced to Jalily, his eyes filled with tears and he said, "I know the work will be begun again!" To him it was inconceivable that his prayers for Mazanderan would go unanswered.

When Jalily retired for the second time and was given a small pension by the Board of Evangeism, he continued as before his voluntary services in the church and in the reading room. This was his life, and he was determined to give his all to his Master. When it was decided that the reading room would be closed on Saturday nights, Jalily changed the time of the meeting in his home from Monday to Saturday. Then a new element was introduced into the program of the meetings. It came to Jalily's mind that when he was a boy he had been given lessons in playing the *tar* and he wondered whether he could now after all these years get back his skill. So he bought a *tar,* and to his delight found that he could bring forth harmony from its strings. Since everything he had belonged to the Lord, the *tar* also must be dedicated to the Lord's service. So when his friends came to the meeting in his home on Saturday night, Jalily asked them to sing hymns while he played an accompaniment on his *tar.* The friends sang lustily the Persian hymns, whether or not they were able to keep close to the tune. And Jalily, transported to another world by the music, put his whole soul into his effort, and for every hymn played the same accompaniment, whether the tune was "Stand up for Jesus" or "Sweet Hour of Prayer." The choir leader in the church might not have been happy over the result, but Jalily and his friends had indeed made a joyful noise unto the Lord and they felt sure he was pleased.

In his latter years, when Jalily's eyesight and physical strength began to fail, and his great consolation was prayer. Ever since his conversion he was a man of prayer. It was his habit for years to remember many of his friends by name in prayer every morning. When he was about seventy years of age he was much attracted to the little son of a missionary friend, and he said he prayed daily for "Stevie" for many years. In 1948 when he was in the School of Evangelism, Jalily read an article in a church paper which told of a remarkable young evangelist who had been greatly used of God in large meetings held in California. This news thrilled him, and from that time he began to pray daily for Billy Graham. Some years later, when Dr. Graham was informed of the faithful prayers of this man of God, he wrote a letter expressing his gratitude, which Jalily deeply appreciated.

Jalily also loved to receive letters from his friends and always replied promptly. His Iranian friends used to say jokingly that Jalily's Persian handwriting was so beautiful no one could read it, and this statement was true for most of his missionary friends. So he bought a little typewriter with English type, and for years used it for his correspondence with his English-speaking friends. His knowledge of English spelling was limited and he often confused English with French. Also, he never mastered the art of typing, nor was his typewriter a model instrument. But the many letters that came from him were, like their author, filled with love to his friends and praise to his Lord. When American soldiers were in Iran during the Second World War, some of the Christian men became close friends of Jalily, and often went to his home. After the war, a few of them continued the friendship by correspondence. Jalily would now and then anounce with joy, "I have received a letter from Clyde from Ohio!"

Several years ago a minister who was preaching on a Sunday morning in the Community Church in Teheran, the members of which were for the most part Americans engaged in government and business projects in Iran, told his congregation the story of the conversion of Jalily. Then he said, "The man about whom I have been speaking is here with us, and I request Mr. Jalily to come to the pulpit and speak for himself." Whereupon a little gentleman with a bald head rose from his seat in the rear of the church and came to the pulpit, and in his quaint English gave his Christian testimony. He told how his former religion had failed to give him peace and joy, and how God had come to him in Christ, and had saved him. "When I was a Muslim," said Jalily, "I thought I knew God, but I did not. I came to know God when I saw him in Christ."

146

If any of those present had previously supposed that the religion of Islam is adequate for those who practice it, or that it is impossible for a devout Muslim to become a Christian, the radiant face of Jalily as he spoke of Christ, and his simple and sincere testimony to the Unseen Power that had changed his life, must certainly have brought to them a new understanding of the uniqueness and indispensability of the Christian faith. For Jalily and all those who like him have come out of Islam into the Christian fellowship, Christ is *the* Way, and there is no other. The Gospel of Christ is *the* power of God to salvation, and "there is no other name under heaven given among men by which we must be saved" (Acts 4:12).

Faithful to the very end of his life on earth, walking on Sundays and Wednesdays through the busy streets of Teheran to the services of the church — despite his increasing blindness, Mahmud Jalily went to receive his crown on January 3, 1969, and his body was laid to rest in the Christian cemetery near the grave of his daughter. He has joined the glorious company of those who by the power of Jesus Christ became more than conquerors.

per
Piszonetting

W: Visit Floyd Sewell.